Conquering the Mysteries and Lies of Grief

Sherry Russell

PublishAmerica
Baltimore

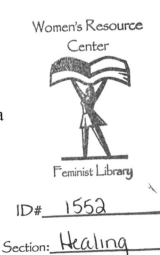

First printing

ISBN: 1-59129-724-9
PUBLISHED BY PUBLISHAMERICA BOOK
PUBLISHERS
www.publishamerica.com
Baltimore

Printed in the United States of America

Dedication

This is for my husband
who offers his love, tenderness, and encouragement
on a daily basis
and to my extraordinary daughter, Tracy.

Acknowledgments

I would like to acknowledge all the people living with loss who have taken me in as a confidante with confidence. They have bestowed upon me their wisdom and shared with me their most intimate fears. Along with those survivors are the lost loves of my own family who have bequeathed me a first-hand education on grief survival.

My path has been an unusual one, sometimes successful and sometimes not. I am so lucky and blessed to have numerous aunts, uncles and cousins that no matter what offer their undying acceptance.

Lastly, I want to acknowledge the woman who almost lost her own life bringing me into this often challenging world. My mother is a strong, will-filled woman marked by a determination streak to survive and claim life for all it has to offer. I am humbly grateful.

Contents

Foreword

This book was in the making for years before the catastrophic September Eleventh event changed all our lives. In dealing with grieving people one on one or in small groups, the same question would always emerge. That question was: "How can I get others to understand no one really knows how I feel? These people say they have had similar experiences to mine but it just isn't the same."

I would conference with them about finding nonjudgmental, supportive people. It isn't as easy as you may think to find those exceptional people who will embrace you as you are and just simply listen. Not rescue you—just listen to you. We would continue on with what they as a griever could do to take an active part in their bereavement. The secret to getting through your grief is knowing how to accept a diligent role in it.

In Grief Workshops, I continue to address that question every time. I ultimately thought if people rationalized why they didn't and couldn't know exactly how another griever feels, then maybe they would quit saying those dreaded few words "I know exactly how you feel." Hence, the primary purpose for this book. Everything was progressing well with the writing until that "day." The writing stopped for a while.

With 9-11, I along with everyone else witnessed and felt the deep painful confusion of grief everywhere I turned. This event caused what I refer to as "group grief." Not only were the survivors coated in their grief, they themselves along with the deceased became victims of an act of terrorism. That "day" has become an unseen thread connecting us with patriotic love for our country and for our neighbors. 9-11 made everyone question who they were and what they were all about. Multitudes of people were shaken to the core of their being. People were questioning their spirituality, their professions, their relationships. People were and are looking for answers to "when will this pain go away?", "what are we going to do now?", "how is this going to affect my life in the future?" and "how can I go on enjoying life when others are hurting so much?"

We have felt enormous sadness, anger, depression, panic, crankiness, impatience, and yes, we have felt the strength of love and spirituality. Even though we experienced this as a group, none of us experienced it the same way. When one of us was still numb, one of us was crying, and yet another of us was screaming.

Grief's talons reached out and invaded us that day, and then it intertwined itself into our lives and changed them forever. Even though we all reacted differently, we did it together and we shared it as Americans.

There is an extensive contrast to the family down the street that loses someone they love to "normal" circumstances. Those normal circumstances might be a death from natural causes, an accident, a long disease, or a crime act. Whatever the reason for the death, it isn't a "group grief" phenomenon. Everyone else's life goes on without hardly a mention of the deceased. The death ordinarily doesn't make the news, and if it does, in two to three days it is quickly lost from memory except to the surviving family. The plights of the surviving family are generally not known. The survivor's phone still rings with oblivious telemarketers asking for the deceased. Bills still arrive in the mailbox every day expecting payment, no matter your problems. The survivor's door bell still rings with a magazine salesman not knowing the heartache that lies inside the home. Co-workers at the survivor's place of employment watch the papers pile up and wonder when they will come back to get it done. Some employers allow three days to "get on with it." Some tell you to take your time but in the back of their mind they are wondering if they are going to have to replace you. This, my friend, is the real world of a grieving family.

This book is a compilation of hundreds of people living with loss. It tells the good, the bad, the pain and the glory—the "isness" of life. It explains what is going on with your body and mind so that you can take an active role in your grief process. It makes sense that the more you understand about what is happening, the better you can take control of your life. Taking part in your grief process allows you to have that control over what you had no control of—the loss of a loved one.

Chapter 1

Lost in Loss

"Indeed they are not gone who have passed beyond
our clasp, for they walk softly in our thoughts by day and
in our dreams by night."
—Author Unknown

He called and said, "I'm worried. I had the strangest thing
happen to me last night. I was alone in my car driving home
when a bright light caught my eye. Suddenly I saw an angel.
She was so bright and beautiful. Odd enough, I wasn't scared
at all. It seemed so natural. I felt the need to get out of the car,
to kneel down and pray. There didn't seem to be anyone else
around. I don't know what happened to everyone. Everything
was so peaceful, and then an angel appeared and told me to get
prepared, for I would be losing the most precious thing I had.
She went on to tell me to tidy things up.

"I don't understand the meaning of all this but I'm afraid
this is about you. I am afraid you are going to die because you
are my most precious thing. I know you are not going to church
on a regular basis anymore. This is a warning—you have to
start back, now. Please be careful. I know something going to
happen to you."

This conversation escalated to an argument. After all, what

had he had to drink and maybe he was just going crazy. He was fanatical about his religion. When you opened his wallet the first picture you would see was one of Jesus. Turning to the next picture you would then see me, his daughter. He was always aggravating me about church, so maybe this was just another stunt. I was so agitated, I couldn't wait to tell someone else about this crazy conversation.

A year to the exact day my father had seen and spoken with his angel, he was dead. This young man in his forties, still a child at heart, fell down a few steps and that was that.

As I was walking up the steps to the hospital, I remembered that heated conversation we had a year ago. I was appreciative that I had shared that talk with someone else. For if I hadn't, I would have concluded that maybe I had gone mad.

What is the truth here? Did the angel really appear to him? I don't know. I just know the lesson here is that the most precious thing you have is really your own life. My father's time was near for whatever reason, and it was time for him to tidy up his affairs. He didn't, but that's another story.

His death plunged me into a complete state of confusion. Odd enough I kept searching for someone to tell me how I was supposed to act. My whole life someone told me how to act and many times what to think—so now what? Who was going to step up to the plate and help me out of this one? No one did.

I ultimately figured out why. Simply no one knows what to anticipate or what to do. Everyone just copies what they have seen others do. Then they secretly and privately hide their true grief. The best acting teacher is by far grief. We all become remarkable actors and actresses. We discover how to conceal the truth to keep others comfortable around us. Meanwhile grief borrows deep into our hearts.

I believe grief is a painful confusion that is endless, unless we try to understand what is happening to us. We must find a way and the strength along with the know-how to create a "new normal."

It took me ten years of anger and confusion to understand this. I hope this book will help you understand a little sooner.

Let's face it, grief is heartache. It is a mysterious emotional, physical, and spiritual puzzle that is solely ours. Unfortunately, sooner or later, every single one of us will be or have already been intimately jarred by loss. What I have learned from interviews with hundreds of people in the throes of grief has guided me to witness grief's extraordinary profoundness. Along with my own experiences, education and the survivor interviews have equipped me well to answer the questions that come up in my Grief Workshops. Some of the questions that come up in the group are: "How can I possibly get through this when the world won't stop and give me time to grasp all of this?", "What should I do next?" and "How do I heal, and if I do heal does that mean I forget my loved one?" It also never fails that at the end of a Workshop, people seem to be waiting in line to talk with me personally. They don't want anyone else to hear this one question: "What on earth is happening to me; am I going crazy?" What they don't know is everyone else standing in line is getting ready to ask that same question. People are searching for answers to help stop the pain. That I can not do. All I can do is offer enough information so people won't suffer for the wrong reasons and will know how to apply this knowledge to help themselves.

Grief is not a school subject, it is not studied or talked about, so when it hits our circle of family or friends, we are completely shocked by the forceful blow it delivers.

I don't know about you, but at a young age I came face to face with the realization no one teaches anything about life-

and-death matters in school. In high school we never talked about it; as a matter of fact, we were sort of taught to ignore it. I remember when a classmate's father committed suicide. It was completely hushed up and we were informed not to talk about it to anyone, especially not to our grieving classmate. So we didn't. We took two steps back from her when she needed us to take two steps forward.

When another classmate's younger brother was killed in an accident, we were told it was O.K. to show sympathy to the family. Then we all started analyzing each other in regards to how we were displaying our sympathy and how we were verbalizing our feelings. Each one of us felt that we knew better how this family might be feeling. But in truth, none of us knows how anyone else is really feeling in grief.

Has grief ever made you feel like you were "faking" it through your everyday life? Could it be others have unintentionally forced you to "fake" it? Maybe it is because everyone tells you not only can they relate but they specifically know what you are going through. They can't wait to tell you they know how you feel, and what's worse they know exactly what you should and must not be doing and/or feeling! It's not like you already don't "should" yourself silly, but now others want to hone in on it, too. And by the way, they don't know how you feel.

Maybe they can relate, and certainly their intention is genuine, but how can anyone possibly know and feel what you discern deep in your heart and what you have stowed away in your mind? There are too many variables that make each grief unique to the survivor. We will examine these variables in another chapter. Meanwhile, you can be thinking about your own personality. Are you personality A or B?

Now, if I were to ask you what comes to mind when someone

mentions the topic of life after death, what would you think? Would you think it means going beyond to your heavenly reward or do you think about karma and returning to this earth for another try? Whatever your thinking may be, grief stamps its own twist on the meaning of life for a survivor after the death of a loved one. For grief, continuing on with life after the death of a loved one is dealing with life after death. Coping with this grief is a painful condition filled with confusion.

This painful condition has both positive and negative features to it, which is one reason why it is so confounding. Believe it or not, while forging through the pain, you have an opportunity for positive change and growth. You will come to a point where you are hopeful for the future, where you have the will to create a new normal and a purpose to carry on. The grief will deepen your capacity to be closer to others and to be nonjudgmental of others in grief.

On the other hand, grief can be laden with despair, disgust, isolation, guilt, anger, shame, and doubt. So, how do you get to the other side of this pain?

First you have to accept the fact that you can not change anything about what has happened. All the hindsight in the world is not going to make a dimple of difference.

The more you focus on what you did wrong rather than what you did right, the longer it will take you to get to the other side of pain. You can not be God. Realize you don't hold the command over who lives and dies.

Second, do realize that experiencing pain is part of being human. Fate doesn't single you out. All people experience loss at some time in their lives. Not all loss is about death. There are many emotional losses one may experience. People have said that losing a loved one is like an amputation with you as the remaining piece. Think about it. If you had to face losing a body limb, you would be facing loss and having to create a "new normal" for yourself. Lost communication with loved ones brings loss. Divorce brings loss into lives. Any time one door in your life is shutting and another is opening, there is a loss of some kind being experienced. So, there are many different layers to loss. Death of a loved one is the ultimate loss with the maximum layers.

Third, do you ever think about your own demise? You too will die someday. You don't know when. You don't know what you will die from. You don't know what will be going on in your life at that time. But you do know you will die at some point. If we accept that truth, then we have to accept the certainty that everybody is going to die at some time. It makes sense that if you know you will die someday, then your loved ones can also die at any time.

Once you have acknowledged these three principles, you can start to manage your grief. After all, you can't deny or hide from it. Grief is there, lurking behind every thought you have, so you might as well confront it. If someone was frightening you, you would do whatever you needed to do in order to protect yourself mentally and physically. If grief frightens you but you don't do anything, it will become your enemy. If you manage it, grief will be your friend and bestow you a gift.

Face it—living with loss is wearisome. To grasp a better understanding, let's for a moment strive to undergo what grief may feel like.

It starts with the life you take for granted. You have no doubt your life is based on a very sturdy foundation. But the death of a loved one causes that foundation to start to crack. You realize how fragile life is. Grief reaches out and grabs you. It surrounds you with a fog that makes you dizzy and numb. Meanwhile the foundation has broken away, and with nothing under your feet to hold you, you fall. You start to tumble into a seemingly bottomless pit. The death of your loved one has shaken you to your core. You know you are falling, yet it feels as if it isn't really happening to you at all. The darkness of the pit feels as if it will invade your soul; you are alone and there is no end in sight. You sense a bulging formation stemming from the side of the pit. The bulge stops your nose-dive fall. For the first time you are now aware of what has happened. Feeling all alone, you look up hoping to see someone. No one appears. Then suddenly out of nowhere, family and friends are gathering and they are peeping down at you. Oh, how they want to help, but they are confused about what to do. As much as they want to help, they are not sure what to do. They are fearful for your safety. They keep calling out to you, instructing you on what you should do. Someone finally gathers the troops. Instead of talking, they are now doing something. They find a thick rope they can use to make a slipshod ladder. Throwing the crude ladder over the side, they see it tumbling towards you. They start bellowing down to you. Your ears are hearing the words being said to you. Your mind is exploding with all this advice. You are confused and numb by what is happening. Slowly, you seize hold of yourself and recognize that you can't change what has happened. You have to accept it and attempt to get out of this pit. At this point, you assess your situation. Feeling paralyzed and still in shock from the fall, you balance on the misshapen lifeless outgrowth under you. You know what you need to do to get out of the pit, and at the same time you panic. Fear sets in. Will the ladder hold your weight? Will they be able to help pull you up? What will happen when you get to the top? Why did your foundation fail you? How will life be now? How will you build a new foundation.

You don't like requesting help; will you be forced to?

Because you've never experienced anything like this, the tools and knowledge you need to manage your feelings are not available. You simply don't know what to do and you don't have any answers. You are terrified to let go of the bumpy ledge because it is what you understand for now. You are fearful that by leaving this ledge you may fall so far down no one would be capable of helping you. It passes through your mind that it would be easier to let go than to fight your way to the top. It takes so much strength and you feel so weak. One moment you ponder you can do it, but the very next you aren't sure. However, being a survivor is built into your personal philosophy of life.

You are not the one that has died; you have been chosen to be the one that must live on. The heavy twine ladder finally arrives. You can barely reach it, but with tenacious effort you clutch it.

Now what? You hear all the advice and instructions being shouted out to you, but they don't know what it is like to be in your position. You will need to take in only the advice you consider may help you. You keep trying to secure your grip and the well-meaning people keep yapping. So much for all the hullabaloo! You need quiet, rest, time.

You finally realize this pilgrimage up this exhausting shaft is going to have to be on your conditions using your own strength. You require light, so you call to them and tell them what you need. They ask how much light, what kind of light. You need them and appreciate them, but they are on your nerves. You are hanging by a thread and they want you to make the decisions! Just give you light. Finally someone listens and actually hears what you are saying. They appreciate your frankness. It is nice for them to know what will really help you, and they promptly get the lights. They shine the lights downward into the pit, spotlighting you, and now you are starting to behold and understand where you are and what you want to accomplish. Making your way up this pit isn't going to be easy, and you may even slip and falter, but you have got to try to scramble out. Slowly and steadily you once again check your handclasp on the ladder rung.

For the first time you feel ready to start leaving that hump of a substructure that you landed on. You are panicky, but there is no other way out. No one can rescue you but you. You set forth up the ladder one rung at a time. Seems to be going acceptably well, but then you slip and find yourself down a few of the rungs that you had so steadfastly climbed. Anger and frustration are setting in. You are trying so hard. You kick the side of the pit. You didn't ask for this life change to happen. Why did your loved one have to die? This is what put you in this pit of despair. They weren't supposed to leave you like this.

You may even be mad at other family and friends because they can't make this all go away, and they really don't know how to help you any more than they are already. No one has any answers. The way they see it is you have the ladder, just climb on out; after all, we are up here rooting for you. You may be exasperated with doctors and hospitals. Let's face it, you are just plain furious with being forced to deal with and focus on this plight.

You didn't ask for it and you don't want it to be this way. You want it like it was. Now you have to figure out how to get to "like it is." Nothing prepared you for this. Pulling it together once again, you start up. You have actually found that the anger gave you a little adrenaline boost. Now you are moving swiftly.

Just as you feel in control, *boom*, the pit starts crumbling dirt down on you. As you sway on the ladder, you start to become depressed thinking that you will never get out of this, so why not just let go? As you silently twist, you hear the call of the people from up above. Once again they are hollering out to you their fears for you and their never-ending advice. But you notice a few people who are sincerely holding out their hands to you. With assuring nods they let you know they are there for you. This gives you the might to equip yourself for this battle.

As you slowly but surely make your way towards the crown of the pit, you commence to notice wee colorful flowers forcing their way through the sides of the pit. You discover that the colors are calming and the shapes fascinating. You cry, yearning for your loved one to be there to see these marvelous flowers. You then decide to stop and rest. While resting, you talk to your loved one and recount your experiences. You tell them how much you miss them. You have now come to terms with the fact that when you get to the top of the pit, life will be different. You have come to accept that you will go on living and that you have responsibilities to others to live a good life, not to just exist.

You are ready to start again. Looking up, you see family and friends. Seeing them assures you and puts a smile on your face. You see the sky in all its magnificence. You are still fearful of what life will offer, but you know you can make it one step at a time. You realize your loved one would want you to relish life and to live life to its fullest.

Your loved one is now gently tucked into your heart, and your memories are amazingly vivid. You are comforted in knowing love never dies. You trust that you will be able to laugh and enjoy life while still keeping your love for the deceased alive with the chosen memories.

You make it to the top. Family and friends rush to support you. They are grateful to have you back, and you are thankful to be back.

Will the pit of grief come and haunt you sometimes? Probably. Will you have fear of slipping back into it? Probably. In years to come will a wave of grief come and go? Yes. Will your love ever die? No. Will you learn to enjoy life? If you want to, you must assuredly will.

So you see, just like climbing out of a deep hole you have to climb your way from what *was* to what *is* in order to recover.

The more you know about what is happening to you in grief, the better you will be able to cope with the changes that occur in your life.

A further look into grief is offered from interviewee number #264:

"I can't breathe. My face is numb. I feel tingling in my arms and hands. I am panicking because I have to go back to work and it has only been a week since my husband died. I know they will all treat me like I'm diseased. The people I thought I could count on don't want me to talk about what happened. They don't understand that I need to talk about it."

This lady will be forced to disguise her genuine feelings. This will ignite a domino effect into other areas of physical grief. This lady has experienced heart palpitations, mood swings, and queasiness.

Later we will look at the cause and effect relationship the stress of losing a loved one has on you physically.

What happens with a lot of us under this kind of painful stress is that we learn to become the instant actor and actress. It starts innocently. You don't want to force a helpful friend or family member into an uncomfortable place, so you become what you think they want you to be. That way they are not disturbed by your sadness. Meanwhile, grief is choking you.

Be assured that many people do have compassion for you. They have a heartfelt awareness for your pain, and they wish to lighten it—which is one reason why these same people want to tell you they know exactly how you feel. They want and need to emotionally touch you. To let you know you are not alone. Little do they know that all you really need from them is to know they are waiting in the wings with support.

These well-intentioned people don't know how you feel, and they can't stop your pain no matter how much they try to rescue you.

Why do you go through so many different yet similar situations and emotions as someone else? Numerous variables make the difference in each person's grief.

There is not one family that is identical to another. There is not one person who is an exact duplicate emotionally and physically. There is not another relationship with all the components of your relationship with the deceased.

In the next chapter we will take a look at reasons why your grief journey is uniquely yours.

Chapter 2

Why Variables Make Your Grief Unique to You

"My sister is eleven years younger than I am. She didn't see Mom the same way I did. Mom's death changed both our lives. My sister and I can't seem to talk about it. We get in arguments over everything. We are just really being affected differently." (Interviewee # 601)

What makes you who you are? Are you a type A personality or a type B? Are you introverted or extroverted? Do you have brothers and/or sisters? Are you the middle child? Are you an only child? How did your parents get along? Were you an orphan?

All these variables make a difference in how you relate to the world, and furthermore how you correlate to your grief. Variables influence the severity, intensity, devotion, and resolution of your grief process. We know and acknowledge that other people may have comparable situations and share similar feelings and emotions, but no one feels exactly like you.

There is no amount of knowledge out there that can prepare us for losing a loved one. There is no amount of training that makes grief easier. However, the more we understand the variables in our life and the more we understand that these variables will produce serenity or obstacles in our grief path, the better we can deal with it. We may agree that we are all indeed so unique.

For example, if you are a type A personality, you are competitive, striving and usually put yourself under pressure. This behavior sometimes is called the coronary-prone behavior pattern!

Try filling in the blanks or making notes on these variables. Think about three of the most emotional losses you have suffered when filling in the blanks.

(handwritten column headings: dio — 32, div — 38, Dad — 44)

Your age at the time of loss — 32, 38, 44
Was it a sudden death — Y, N, ~
Was it a long terminal illness — nl, Y, y
Was it an accidental death — N, N, N
Was it a violent death — N, N, N
Are you male or female — F
What is your religion — Epis c
What is your cultural background — wh mid class
How is your health — good
What is your relationship to deceased — stu, wife, daughter
How prepared were you for the death — N, Y, nl
Do you have good family communications — Y, Y, y
Do you have a support system — Y, Y, y
Are your financial resources adequate — Y, Y
Was death discussed before loved one died — N, N, N
Did deceased pre-plan their arrangements — N, N, Y
Did you get a chance to say "good-bye" — Y, Y, N

If you filled in the blanks, you are starting to see why and how your grief path has to be different from anyone else's. The impact of all these variables on the loss conclude how we will cope and adjust to our life events.

In your initial reaction to the loss, you experience various emotions. These emotional reactions to your loss may include shock, numbness, confusion, fear, anger, resentment, and guilt. These emotions coupled with the variables trigger the fight or flight response. The variables will decide why you react in a different way than someone else in the fight or flight response.

Fight or flight is a physical and psychological response to a threat. Our fears are out of proportion and our thinking is distorted.

Once the fight or flight reaction is activated, our body reacts in many ways. Keep in mind the body is reacting to this as an automatic, involuntary response. In this response an area of the brain stem releases an increased quantity of norepinephrine, which in turn causes the adrenal glands to release more adrenaline. You experience a faster heart rate, pulse rate and respiration rate. In addition, you get a release of blood sugar, lactic acid, and other chemicals.

Feelings of apprehension, fear, and impending doom are all common. Other noticeable changes include dilated coronary arteries, higher blood pressure, increase in muscle tension, moisture on the skin, dilated pupils, dilation of the bronchial tubes, hydrochloraic acid secreted into the stomach, glucose released from the liver, and increase in basal metabolic rate. The white blood cells are lowered, which decreases the effectiveness of the immune system, which may make you vulnerable to disease-causing bacterium and degenerative disease. So as you see, a lot is going on in your body. All most people in grief perceive is that they just simply feel miserable!

Interviewee # 159 related her experience about fight or flight. Her mother in law was living with her and her husband. The mother-in-law was very ill but still somewhat mobile. She needed help getting to go the bathroom, so she summoned her son. He walked her to the bathroom, and he then went back to watching his television show.

Almost an hour had passed, and he realized his mother had not called for him to walk her back to bed. He went to the bathroom door and called out her name. Not hearing anything, he frantically yelled for his wife. He didn't want to embarrass his mother by marching in on her in private moments. His wife gingerly opened the door to the bathroom. She was stunned to find her mother-in-law on the cold floor, dead. Her husband froze. He stood numb.

When the wife asked her husband to make the necessary phone calls, he walked past the phone in the kitchen and went out the side door. After making the essential calls, she nervously waited for her husband to return home. She ultimately made decisions on her own and was exceedingly resentful towards her husband. She thought him to be uncaring and disrespectful. In reality he plainly took flight rather than fight. He was fearful and anxiety-ridden, which put him into the fight or flight reaction. He became focused on his short-term survival, not the long-term consequences.

Another example of how one of these variables may make your grieving process solely yours:

A clinical research showed that when there is advance warning of the death, the grief process may be helped. Colin Parkes, a psychiatrist, studied sixty-eight widows and widowers. His study showed that the reaction of those who had at least two weeks warning before the impending death was less severe and not as drawn out as those who had little or no advance warning. His study showed these people were less depressed, less anxious, and less self-blaming than survivors who were shocked by the death of a loved one.

Colin Parkes likewise took into consideration the multitudes of variables that exist in determining and shaping a person's grief response. Parkes's studied such questions as how survivors attempt to establish connections to others following bereavement. Parkes identified three components as central to grief work:

Preoccupation with thoughts of the deceased person.
Repeatedly going over the loss experience in one's mind.
Attempts to explain the loss or make some sense of the death.

Another variable that sets your grief apart is simply whether you are male or female. Men and women grieve differently. One way they contrast is in the freedom to express their grief.

I talked with a husband and wife (interviewees #936 and 937) who lost their twenty-year-old daughter to a car accident. The daughter had come home from attending college in another town for vacation. She was taking a nap when a friend called and persuaded her to go shopping. Even though she was tired, her friend convinced her to go to the mall. The mall was only twenty minutes away and they decided they wouldn't be long. The mother said she had experienced an eerie feeling all day that day. The mother recalled that her daughter had cheerfully helped around the house earlier that day and that was something she never did. The mother said the last words her daughter said were: "I'll be back by nine. I love you, Mom."

It had been eleven months since the accidental death of their daughter, and their marriage was suffering. The wife was reliving the final day over and over. She kept remarking if only she had voiced that weird anxiety she had felt, maybe the daughter wouldn't have gotten into the car. The mother had to find a way to come to terms with the facts: she can't be God and she too will die someday. Once she accepted these two facts, she stopped second-guessing and questioning.

The husband was upset that his wife would not let go of "that" day. He felt like he should "fix" his wife. Make her all better. Make their life all better. He desperately wanted to stop or at least ease her pain, but he couldn't. What made it worse was she persistently told him about her excruciating suffering. That made him feel even more out of control. After all, in his generation, the man was supposed to take care of his family. Keep them safe. Keep them happy. Yet now his daughter was dead and his wife was broken-hearted. He didn't understand his wife's need to discuss the last time they saw their daughter or the accident that caused the death. He was interpreting this as criticism from his wife. His perspective was: the accident happened; my daughter is gone; nothing is ever going to bring her back; talking about it isn't going to help; why can't we at least pretend to go on with our life?

Her perspective was: I need to talk with you about my anger, my fear, and my inconceivable heartache; I want you to open up to me; I need to make sense of this and I need you to validate my feelings. The wife believed the husband must not have felt the deep pain she did. She wanted him to feel the sad and hurtful pain. She needed him to feel her pain. She was judging him in his grief and he was judging her. They were openly hostile towards each other. Every wee circumstance was adding fuel to this already blazing fire.

Once husband and wife realized and acknowledged that they both were in deep grief, they reacted differently to it. Now they could start to communicate again. Their interaction began to tear down the barriers each one had put up and permitted them to work together as a team in their grief.

So many couples are woefully torn apart when the dynamics

of the family changes following a death. The death detonates an avalanche of emotions for each person, and each person is looking for the other one to feel and act a certain way. If only people would acknowledge the variable factors and realize each person just needs to be listened to and not judged.

Many women want to analyze the death. They need to dissect every minute and attempt to discover clues to put it all together. They want to analyze what happened before, during, and after the death. Women are more demonstrative and unguarded with their emotions. They want to talk about the death and what happened and what could have happened and maybe what happened over and over and then over again. Women need to be verbal. Women are perceptive and cope outwardly. Many women will reach forth for support and readily disclose their feelings. They cry.

Men see the overall situation. Men tend to keep their thoughts inside. Reserving their feelings inside, sometimes a man may just shut down. Men are disposed to being analytical about the death. "Just the facts, ma'am" is what the men want to deal with. Men have an inclination to moan and sigh rather than outright cry. Men have a penchant to avoid feelings or outwardly displaying emotions in a public situation. Sometimes, they may even seem to be more angry than brokenhearted at the death. Men are less likely to seek support from others, especially in a group format. Whenever a man braves coming to one of my Grief Workshops, as a rule I let him know how courageous he was for coming in and I encourage him to participate, if and only if he feels inclined.

You have to keep in mind that sometimes men find showing their grief to be embarrassing. In general, men will be apt to put their feelings into action. They will focus on accomplishing something or taking an action in regards to the death.

When we as women or men suffer a loss, we experience it on an emotional, physical, and spiritual level. Along with the variables, we proceed to deposit our personal autograph on our grief. Just like the slant of the letters formed are different in everyone's handwriting, so is the slant we put on setting up our boundaries.

We set physical and emotional boundaries. These boundaries define you from others. With the husband and wife, their boundaries were different. The physical boundary lets others know when they are violating your space. It lets others appreciate when you are comfortable being with them. The wife's physical boundary kept saying to her husband: "come hug me, reassure me." His physical boundary was saying: "don't get too close." Her emotional boundary was set for communication and reaching out. His emotional boundary was shut to her. She emotionally desired him to be a tower of strength, but he was internally experiencing and dealing emotionally with his own grief.

The above-mentioned couple's grief was caused by a sudden accident. They never saw their daughter alive again once she left their house. Even though I believe men and women grieve differently, let me now say this: some women will grieve in a traditionally masculine way and some men will grieve in a traditionally feminine way. Remember it depends on all your variables. There are no facts to grieving.

Chapter 3

Phases, Stages, and Mazes

"If but one message I may leave behind,
One single word of courage for my kind,
It would be this—Oh, brother, sister, friend,
Whatever life may bring, what God may send,
No matter whether clouds lift soon or late,
Take heart and wait.
Despair may tangle darkly at your feet,
Your faith be dimmed, and hope, once cool and sweet,
Be lost; but suddenly above a hill,
A heavenly lamp, set on a heavenly sill
Will shine for you and point the way to go,
How well I know.
For I have waited throughout the dark, and I
Have seen a star rise in the blackest sky
Repeatedly—it has not failed me yet.
And I have learned God never will forget
To light His lamp. If we but wait for it,
It will be lit."

—Grace Noll Crowell

No matter your type of grief, no matter the variables that make your grief different from someone else's, you will go through what some people call phases or stages.

The understanding of these phases allows you to give yourself a break. You will encounter many of these phases/stages as you work through your grief. The grief work is like a bridge. On one side you have *what used to be* and on the other you have *what now exists*. Getting over the bridge is the grief work. It is the enduring of the phases/stages part. You may stumble and tumble through some of these phases, and you may not. You may go through several of them at the same time. If the person you lost went through a long illness, you may have gone through many of these phases/stages while the person was still living.

Part of the suffering through these phases/stages is the wrestling you are doing with trying to put your life back together. Many people I have spoken with desperately longed for the day they would wake up and grief would be gone. They found out as most people do that impatience does not partner well with your grief.

Most people are impatient because they want to control and shape their grief the way they want. How can you control a formless mass like grief? Grief is without form. Grief prescribes its own boundaries and doesn't consult you to see if it gets a "yes" vote for you to be miserable today. One explanation for why we become so tormented is that by nature we are creatures of control, even though most people will shy away from being called a controller. Take a closer look and I think you will understand why I say this.

We like to control and/or manage as many of the elements in our life as possible. We like to control where we live, what we eat and most likely what someone else eats, too. We control where our children go to school, what they wear, and we try to control who their friends are. We not only want to control ourselves, but we want to control those around us! The list of control issues is endless. So I think we can agree that we like to control or at least have control of our lives. If you accept this, then it will be easier for you to embrace why it is so laborious to acknowledge and welcome a new reality. Some people I have spoken with would prefer me to say they are disciplined people. Word games—control or discipline—it doesn't matter what you call it, for when a death happens, it will thump you in the head and knock you right off your control or discipline center.

Grief will seize control of your life; however, by understanding these phases/stages, you can negotiate through the winding, thicket-filled journey of grief and come to the conclusion that you can capture back the controls in your life.

I don't call what we go through phases or stages. I instead devised a maze. My maze is filled with stepping stones. Even though these stones are laid throughout the maze, there needs to be an awareness that sometimes you can step on two or more at a time. Also there are times when you step back rather than forward. Finally you will come out on the other side of this maze with a tolerant understanding for your grief.

I named the first stone "anguish." Why? Simply, grief is exhausting. It is miserable. It is heartache. Remember that grief hits you mentally, physically, and spiritually. So all at once you are dealing with what is going on in your head, all the physical symptoms in your body, along with the deep hurt and loss in your heart. Nothing is easy about that. Even though grief is a normal reaction to your loss, it is the most devastating situation you will ever deal with. So, you have to conclude, grief is going to hurt. While you are on "anguish" step, you may feel like you need to pinch yourself and wake up. It is as though a dream. You make decisions. You see out of eyes that wonder if they are focusing right. You may make it through the day, through communicating with friends and family, maybe even through work. But you are numb and not really able to focus. We might have to tell people we can't remember a detail or we just can't get our mind to work. Your mind can only handle so much, so when you have a numbness come over you, your mind is just protecting you from the full-blown punch of grief.

The second step I call "amazement." We are amazed at the power of our emotions. This emotional abyss is shocking to us. One minute we are fine and the next we think we have gone crazy. We are afraid to share our feelings with other people for fear of being judged—or worse, for fear they may confirm that yes, we just might be nuts! Don't worry, you are not crazy—you are experiencing grief. There is a lot of confusion, doubt, anger, and fear, and many times these emotions are overlapping one another. With so much going on, no wonder so many of us think we are going crazy!

A third step I call "abandonment." We need to learn that fighting grief is not going to get us anywhere. To stay stuck in grief should not be considered an alternative. It doesn't prove your love for the deceased. It just proves you have made a relationship with your grief. We have to be careful not to confuse misery with love. I have had many men, women, and children tell me they are afraid to even laugh because others may think they don't hurt anymore. Some of these people told me they were afraid of criticism from family and friends. Some told me they just couldn't laugh because they never wanted to forget their pain. In talking with many hundreds of people, I have never met one that said "I'm over it so now I can laugh." None of us ever get over it. We get through it. We get to the point of "I can deal with how life is now rather than fight for how life used to be." Once that truism happens we can go on living, but we don't get over it. So when a person tells me they don't ever want to laugh again, I think we need to talk about an attitude adjustment! First of all, you didn't die. Whether you like it or not, you weren't chosen to die—you were chosen to live. Live being the operative word here. You have many responsibilities to other people who are living. You can't just quit life! On the other hand, I guess you could allow yourself to get sucked down the pit by your grief. What would that accomplish? It would be another loss, but it would be the worst kind of loss—a living person not "living." It is one thing to pull into your "shell" every once in a while to regroup, and it is another to decide to be an empty shell bobbing through the remainder of your life. If you don't want to think about what that does to your existence, then think what that would do to everyone else around you. Life is never fair, but life is to be lived. When you abandon yourself to your grief, you finally come to grips with knowing you have to make it through the pain of grief to get to the other side. The other side of this pain is your new reality. Even though you don't know what reality awaits you at the other side of the pain, by abandoning yourself to it you have power over it. I know that sounds odd. That giving into your pain gives you authority over your grief. But by abandoning yourself to this pain, you recognize that this grief work can't be short cut. It gives you the power to work through it and to experience all of it. Abandoning yourself gives you the power to accept the terms with the variables that make your grief unique. We all at some time have to decide to give into it and know that we are not going crazy, we are just allowing ourselves to feel every aspect of our grief. Abandoning to our grief blasts the blocks that stop our path. It allows us to "get with the flow." We can continue to feel, grow, understand, and to let go of "what was."

Another stone in my maze is called "assistance." We need assistance. Even though no one can truly feel our pain, we need people to listen to us. We need people to be nonjudgmental of us. We need people to allow us to grieve and yet be close at hand. A lot of us don't want assistance because we are afraid that what we say to someone else just may come back to bite us on the fanny one day. How many times have you emotionally opened up to a friend or a family member only to have it used against you at some time? You are very fortunate if that has never happened to you. My experience has been that some unbelievable things can come out of a loved one's mouth in an argument! In grief, you need someone that you can trust will never spit back words. Sometimes, it pays to pay. In other words, if you have feelings that you just can't share with anyone in your life for fear of judgment or for fear you will be hearing it again, then pay a counselor. You can come clean with a counselor and you can be assured it will not come back to haunt you.

This is an example of a lady who went outside her circle to talk about her distress:

Interviewee # 71: "My seventeen-year-old daughter was very ill with cancer. She had been sick for four years. It got to a point where she couldn't keep anything down. I was constantly having to clean her up. Her pain was getting worse. Secretly I wished it would all be over. I have hated myself for so long for thinking that way. I feel so selfish. I was so tired all the time. My other children felt like I was ignoring them. I just couldn't handle it all. Sometimes I would feel like screaming when I had to get up in the middle of the night to change the bedsheets one more time. My whole life became about taking care of her and worrying about what would happen next. I even had to stop working, so bills are another matter that I am dealing with now. I feel so guilty. I am so sorry for having those feelings. I just had no hope."

This mother was so distraught over her anger and her fear at her daughter's illness and then resentful of the hardship the daughter's illness brought to the family's life. This mother couldn't get the thoughts she had about her daughter's life-and-death situation out of her mind. She believed her family would be hurt and ashamed if she told them her real feelings about wishing that her daughter's nightmare would just end. She believed her family would judge her love for her daughter not to be as deep as it was. This mother was in wretched pain. She needed to feel free to talk about her feelings with someone that would not be connected to her day-to-day life. This mom needed to be assured and to know that it was okay to be human and that her anxiety and fear did not diminish the love she felt for her daughter.

When you feel you aren't sure of the repercussions of your words to another, find someone outside of your circle of family and friends to talk with, someone you can trust to be nonjudgmental.

The next stone in my maze is the "attempt" stone. It is the stone representing the effort it takes to get through this maze. As we know, grief is not agreeable. It holds many lessons for us. Sometimes we learn a lesson and advance two steps forward. Oops—sometimes we don't and back we go. Getting through your grief is a considerable undertaking. It is like driving through the fog in the mountains. You slow down, turn on your fog lights, and you still can't see. So you pull over and wait. Then when the fog starts to lift, you inch your way until you get through the mist. When you are pain-racked with grief, sometimes you just need to stop and rest and then inch your way to the other side of it.

The last step inside my maze is simply the "advance" stone. This stone allows you to advance out of the maze. To go forward with life. You intermesh your love and memories of the deceased and your present life together. They now go hand in hand. Instead of your life being torn into two pieces—one being the grief you hold inward and the other being the person you put out to the world—you are now one. You start to be yourself again. As your life progresses and changes into the new normal, you establish a new-sprung foundation partially built with your loved one's memories in mind.

There is one last step. It is right outside the maze. It is called "adoration." It is a step of freedom. It opens up your memories and awakens you to the fact that even though your loved one isn't in this physical world, your love for them is still real and survived the death. This step allows you to talk to your loved one while you are on your way to work in the morning. It is the step that allows you to smile when you hear a piece of music your loved one rocked and swayed to. It is the step that allows you to pay homage to those you lost and to those still here. It is the step that nourishes you through the rest of our life.

To recap, my maze has seven "A" stones to get you through your grief work—anguish, amazement, abandonment, assistance, attempt, advance, and adoration. As you wander around the path on these stepping stones, you will find your way and you will get to the other side. Yes, life does get better. Working your way through your grief and time allow you to get authority over your pain and weave it into your life in an adapted position so you can go on living a fruitful life.

In 1969, Elizabeth Kubler-Ross, M.D., a psychiatrist, wrote *On Death and Dying*. She has spent most of her life working with the dying. While Kubler-Ross was working in a New York hospital, she became dismayed by the treatment of dying patients. She stated that these dying patients were shunned and abused. She felt that no one was honest with these patients. Kubler-Ross sat with terminal patients and listed and interviewed them. She then started giving lectures about what these dying patients told her they were going through. Kubler-Ross has written over twenty books on the subject of death and dying. In her research she saw a pattern emerging that she expressed in the way of stages. These stages start when the patient is first aware of his/her terminal illness. Kubler-Ross believes that these stages are universal. She identified the following stages a terminally ill person goes through—not the survivor. However, over the next twenty-eight years these stages became recognized by professionals as stages of a grieving survivor or a survivor of a deep emotional loss. The stages are:

Shock and Denial: This is a temporary shock response to bad news. This allows people time to develop their defenses.

Anger or resentment: "Why me?" Blame directed against the loved one, doctor, hospital, God. You may feel like others don't care. Other people are enjoying life while you experience pain.

Bargaining: Kubler-Ross calls this a brief period. One that is a period of temporary truce.

Depression: The person admits this has happened and the acknowledgment brings depression.

Acceptance: Kubler-Ross says this is a time of facing the death calmly.

Kubler-Ross makes a point that hope is an important aspect of all the stages. A person's hope can help him/her through difficult times.

There are some criticisms of these stages. The University of Kentucky did a presentation on Kubler-Ross and other approaches. They addressed some of the criticisms of Kubler-Ross's stages. One criticism was that the actual term of stages implies a set order of conditions, that there is no evidence that people go through these stages in this order. Since the theory has become very well-known, patients may rush themselves, or may be pressured by family members, to move through the stages. It was agreed that Kubler-Ross had an impact on society and got us thinking about coping with death. The presentation brought out that half of the problems with the Kubler-Ross model are in society's interpretation and misuse of her research.

Dr. Colin Parkes, a social psychiatrist and author of *Bereavement in Adult Life*, recognized these as stages:

Disbelief: feelings of numbness or shock
Yearning: you want your loved one back
Disorganization and despair: confusion and gloom set in
Re-organization: create a new normal

Dr. Erich Lindemann, a pioneer in the study of grief management, came to the United States in 1927. In 1937 he became Professor of Psychiatry at Harvard University.

Dr. Lindemann, while directing clinical work at Massachusetts General Hospital, specialized in research with patients suffering from mental and physical illness induced by grief and sorrow. Many of these bereaved people developed severe sickness or depression years after the loss of a loved one. His study showed that the stages he defined last from two to five years. His stages were:

Somatic Distress: It can last in waves of twenty minutes to an hour. You can have symptoms such as a tightness in the throat, choking and shortness of breath, a need to sigh, an empty feeling in the abdomen, a lack of muscular power.

Hallucinations: A preoccupation with the deceased. You may experience a sense of unreality. Can actually see the decreased person. May see shadows and/or hear voices.

Guilt: Somehow you feel you failed to do the right thing.

Hostile reactions: You experience anger. You may extinguish yourself from friends. Isolation.

Loss of patterns of conduct: You become restless, aimless, and cannot concentrate.

Identification with the deceased: You may assume traits of the deceased. May even take on symptoms of the deceased's last illness.

He also acknowledged there were many different types of grief, such as:

Anticipatory Grief: The presence of grief in anticipation of the death.

Acute Grief: Intense immediate phase after the death or loss of someone that happens suddenly.

Normal Grief: The period of time that it takes to resolve the loss.

Exaggerated Grief: Going to extremes.

Delayed Grief: This may be caused by mood-altering medications or having to put your own things aside in order to keep others together.

Unresolved Grief: This is almost always about undelivered communication of an emotional nature.

Abbreviated Grief: Immediate replacement of the lost person. An example of this would someone who becomes involved in a relationship right away after the death of a spouse.

Dr. Lindemann found that to repress feelings of grief may lead to abnormal relations in your life later on.

In my interviews, many people, especially in the age range over forty, agreed that they had been taught that crying was a weakness, especially for the men. They said that most of them had been told to "take it on the chin" and "keep a stiff upper lip." In my workshops I always ask people if they have ever kissed anybody with a "stiff upper lip." It just wouldn't be very reassuring, would it? That stiff lip would hide the emotion and message behind the kiss. So why should we hide the emotion in regards to loss? Mental health professionals have now established that expression of grief is a healing process. If you repress this sadness, you will end up loading up an imaginary bag of woes, carrying it into many other areas of your life, and unloading it on unsuspecting people all through your relationships.

After experiencing a death of a loved one, you must launch your grief work in order to discover what will be. Whether you want to call it a stage, a phase, or a maze, you will go through many different twist and turns. There is no turning back the clock. That clock just keeps on ticking. Nothing stands still, no matter how much you desire it.

"Why won't the world just stop? I just need to regroup. You won't believe what happened today. I got a call from the ambulance company wanting to know when I was going to pay the bill. I didn't know that was separate from all the hospital bills I am trying to pay. It just really hurt and it made me mad they would call. I feel like everybody wants something from me, and by the way, what is with all this probate stuff? I don't have a lawyer, now I guess I'll have to get one. Now this means one more person will need answers from me. I need time."

This interviewee (#303) was so distraught by the avalanche of endless questions and things to do. Sometimes the world seems hard and cold, especially when you are the survivor. Creditors still want to be paid and rightfully so. People still need answers to their questions in order to help you. Even the IRS wants the last tax return filed. While you and I may think the death of a loved one is reason to stop the world if only for a moment, others find it an inexcusable reason. That may seem cruel, but that is the way it is. The bottom line is no one other than you really understands or has the time to deeply care about where you are in your grief. No matter how much someone else wants to help, they have a life to live, too. It is up to you to take an active part in your grief. The way to start is by understanding how you may encounter some of these stages, phases, or mazes along the way in your grief work. Once again, the more information and understanding you have of your situation, the better you are to confront it.

This grief work thrusts you onto a journey of phases, stages, and mazes that you didn't ask for. Your loved one went on a journey that no longer confines him/her to this earth. Your journey is full of gravity. As you work your way through this journey, some of the weightiness will be lost along the way. Even once you have gotten through it and arrive at the other side of your pain, waves of grief will come over you at times. But now you will be more prepared for these waves and you can anticipate your weakest times, such as anniversaries, birthdays, the death date, and other special or specific dates. We have established that variables make your grief strictly unique to you. We also know that there are many aspects to grief that come in the form of phases/stages. So next we will look at how the stresses of grief can have a domino effect on everything else in your life, starting from the day the loss happened and continuing for the rest of your life.

Chapter 4

Stress: The Domino Effect of Grief

"Everything in my life came about because I am as I am."
—C.G. Jung

Have you ever watched someone put hours into building and balancing dozens of dominoes? Then oh so carefully they give a little nudge to the first domino to set the rest in motion. Stress is the same way. Stress bumps into every area of your life just like the domino that delicately jars the one behind it into action. It affects your relationships, your health, your employment, your physical and spiritual well-being. In your grief you encounter elephant-size stress that triggers your symptoms into an exaggerated level.

Since loss is recognized as the biggest stressor you can have, you may have gotten GAS from it. GAS is General Adaptation Syndrome.

The theory of GAS came from a pioneer in research on stress. Dr. Hans Selye, considered to be the founder of this concept, defined stress as the non-specific response of the body to any demands made upon it. He went on to explain that each demand made on the body is unique and each has a definite response. He found that the accumulation of stresses, if intense enough, would cause physical disorders.

As a medical student Hans Selye noticed that patients in the early stages of infectious disease showed similar symptoms. These symptoms seemed to show up in the patients regardless of the type of disease they had. His research showed that certain changes take place within the body during stress.

Well, you're wondering what this has to do with you. Let me explain a little more about GAS. Hans Selye also showed that if the emotional and physical stress was left untreated it would lead to infection, illness, and disease. GAS is thought to be the main reason why stress is such an abundant source of health problems. In Hans Selye's General Adaptation Syndrome, he identified each stage. He assigned a name for these three common responses patients experienced. They were the following:

Stage 1. *Alarm Reaction:* Any physical or mental trauma will trigger an immediate set of reactions that combat the stress. The immune system is at first depressed and then the normal levels of resistance are lowered. This makes you more susceptible to infection and disease.

Stage 2. *Resistance:* We think we are immune to the stress. We take it in stride as if we have adapted to it. But our immune system works overtime during this period of resistance.

Stage 3. *Exhaustion:* We run out of all our reserves. Our energy level is low and our immunity system is down. Our mental resources suffer.

So, as you are starting to see, stress is like your own personal explosive device. In this first stage of GAS, the alarm reaction the body releases adrenaline to combat the stress and to stay in control. In Chapter Two we talked about the fight or flight response. What happens in this response is your muscles tense up, you can hear your heartbeat, you worry you might be having a heart attack, your eyes dilate, and you may also experience nausea from your stomach tensing up.

In the second stage, resistance or adaptation, your body is responding to long-term protection. It secretes more hormones that increase blood sugar levels to keep the energy level up and to raise the blood pressure. If the stress whether real or imaginary keeps you in this stage too long, you can become ill.

In the last stage, exhaustion, you experience adrenal exhaustion. The blood sugar levels decrease as the adrenals become depleted. This will lead to continuing mental and physical exhaustion and illness. One study showed that reduced immunity makes the body more susceptible to everything from getting colds to cancer. Cancer is significantly higher among people who have suffered the death of a spouse in the previous year.

Interviewee #32: "When my wife and I went to the funeral home to make arrangements, it was because I had cancer. The doctor told me he didn't know how long I would have to live. I have to admit, I was feeling sorry for myself much of the time, especially when I was going through treatment. My wife stayed at home with me most of the time. When she went out it was to get something for me or to take me somewhere. I guess she didn't have any pleasures in her life during this time. She was offered help, but I didn't want anybody else there. No one could have convinced me that she could possibly die before me. No one could have changed my mind about my insistence on her help and only her help. What a fool I was not to see what this was doing to her. She was the caregiver and I was the care-taker. My illness took it all out of her. When I started doing better, it seemed like that is when she let her guard down and just died."

Even though his wife did not die from stress itself, her body lost all its resistance. She died of immune deficiency. It is important that we understand the nitty gritty about how bad stress affects you. The knowledge takes the fear out it and arms you with the ability to reason your way through it or to know it is a good thing to see your doctor.

In reality we have to have some stress in our life. Stress is not always bad. Stress can be very good. Stress stimulates you and increases your level of alertness. Life would be very tedious if we didn't have any stress. In an ordinary day with ordinary stress you can respond fifty to one hundred times to a moderate fight or flight. Even with ordinary stress, if the tension starts to build you can improve your overall well-being with relaxation and stress-management techniques. This increases your changes of living a disease-free life!

When experiencing a deep emotional loss like the death of a loved one, stress becomes unpleasant and exhausting. First there is the deep emotional loss that sets you off on a turning point in your life. Then there is a lack of clarity about what will happen next. Lastly, with all these changes and demands being made on you, the stretch of time that this will continue is unsure. All of this upheaval causes stress to be a menacing intruder on your ability to perform realistically. This type of stress can jeopardize your health.

As the different variables determine how your grief is different from others, these variables also affect how you react to stress.

To further dissect stress, let's look at short-term stress and long-term stress. When stress is grabbing you by the back of the neck, come back to these pages and circle the symptoms you are feeling. Better yet, keep a log. It doesn't have to be in a fancy journal. A pad of paper will do. You will find, as others have, you are not alone in having these kind of symptoms and you are not crazy. Since more people than you might think experience so many of these symptoms, no need for you to try and hide what you are going through.

Just as we found out that phases can overlap one another, you can also experience multiple symptoms of stress. Unfortunately, sometimes when you are under the most stress, your capacity to recognize what is happening will often diminish. Sort of like the "you can't see the forest for the trees" syndrome.

Some of the physical symptoms you may get from short-term stress are the following: faster heartbeat, nausea, feel like you can't get your breath, increased sweating, cold hands and feet, tense muscles, need to urinate often, diarrhea. When you are experiencing these symptoms, you may also have foggy judgment, confusion in making decisions, defensive attitude, low self-esteem, irritableness, anger, and an overall feeling of general frustration.

When your body is exposed to stress for a longer period of time, you may also have a change in appetite, unexplained back pain, other unexplained aches and pains, headaches, stomach problems, skin eruptions, and fatigue. You also may worry too much, feel intense anxiety, feel like you can't make decisions, feel out of control, experience frequent mood changes, become depressed, have difficulty sleeping, overeat, and rely more on medications or alcohol.

Under long-term stress that keeps you in the fight or flight response, you may actually be clogging arteries by the fat and cholesterol released by the body during the response. This kind of stress may also reveal itself as depression, severe headaches, sleeplessness, ulcers, asthma, blurred vision, errors in judging distance, reduced creativity, lack of concentration, living in the past, and diminished sense of the meaning of life.

People around you may even notice that you have started talking too fast or too loud, that you have facial twitches, that you become irrational, overly emotional, that you have become accident- prone, and you neglect your personal appearance.

In the last chapter we talked about being creatures of control. Well, when you are experiencing many of the symptoms just listed, you just might see why you could feel out of control. This kind of stress brings forth much anxiety. Dr. Albert Ellis, who wrote *Reason and Emotion in Psychotherapy,* started the cognitive-behavior movement in psychotherapy. Ellis started practicing this new therapy in 1955. By the seventies, the above-mentioned book had come to help many therapists and laypeople. Why am I telling you all this? To get back to anxiety. Dr. Ellis listed five main unrealistic desires and beliefs that cause anxiety. They are:

– The desire always to have the love and admiration of all people important to you. This is unrealistic because you have no control over other people's minds. They can have bad days, see things in odd ways, make mistakes or be plain disagreeable and awkward.

– The desire to be thoroughly competent at all times. This is unrealistic because you only achieve competence at a new level by making mistakes. Everybody has bad days and makes mistakes.

– The belief that external factors cause all misfortune. Often negative events can be caused by your own negative attitudes. Similarly your own negative attitudes can cause you to view neutral events negatively. Someone else might find something positive in something you view as a problem.

– The desire that events should always turn out the way that you want them to, and that people should always do what you want. Other people have their own agendas and do what they want to do.

– The belief that past bad experience will inevitably control what will happen in the future. You can very often improve or change things if you try hard enough or look at things in a different way.

Anxiety can make you feel like you are living in constant fear. J.A. Froude said, "Fear is the parent of cruelty." For anyone living now or who lived in the past with great anxiety knows the meaning of that sentence.

Are you under stress now? Hopefully by reading this chapter you will be able to tally up the symptoms and take some action. You can avoid major problems by being aware of what is going on with you. Remember, you can't count on someone else to keep you up to date on your mental and physical well-being. You have to take an active part in assessing yourself. If you surround yourself with nonjudgmental people, you can talk with them about these symptoms and let them tell you what they see going on with you through their eyes.

What can you do to help yourself? Here is a list of suggestions you may find helpful, and guess what—they work!

Go to your doctor. Get checked for any hidden illnesses.

Decisions: Don't make any major decisions if at all possible. There is too much going on. Wait on the big stuff if you can. If not, certainly get some feedback for the decision you are making.

Exercise. Exercise is nature's tranquilizer. It breaks up the stress patterns in the body. You don't have to exercise intensely. You don't have to go to a gym. Just take a walk for twenty minutes, especially when the sun is out. This is an instant stress tamer.

Make a list of all the things you need to get done. Make one list with today's items to do. Make a list with what needs to be done the rest of the week. Try to prioritize these lists. Which ones really must be done? Are there some items you can delegate to someone else?

Only do what you want to do. When people call you and you don't feel like talking, don't. Thank them for calling and let them know this is not a good time but the next time they call might be. If they don't understand, find that nonjudgmental person. Remember, this is not anyone else's grief but yours. You don't need to make others feel comfortable. You don't need to be an actor/actress so others are assured you are okay. Why would you be okay? You are getting through it, but you haven't created that new normal yet, and stress is beating you up.

Express yourself. If you hold it all in, you will bust. If you are having a bad hour, day, or week, just explain by telling others you are having a hard time dealing with yourself. You realize they might have trouble dealing with you. Be honest. If someone says something completely stupid to you, just let them know you appreciate their thought but that isn't the way it is. If people take two steps back from you, they are not the right ones to have around you at this time. You need those nonjudgmental people who will take two steps forward.

Take charge where you can. Make decisions that are right for you. Interviewee #92 relayed this:

"The first Christmas my husband was gone, my two

adult children decided Christmas customs would go on as usual. I just wasn't up to it and I knew it. I hated telling them there would be no tree at my house this year. There would not be a big dinner. Christmas would not be as usual. At first I thought I should go on with how it used to be, but then I thought, *why do I want to put all that pressure on myself?* So I didn't. They accepted it. We got through Christmas."

Writing down the pros and cons of a decision you need may make it easier for you. Also if you imagine that the decision you make will only affect you and no one else, it may make it clear to you what you need to do.

Just say no. Interviewee #62 shared this:

"My good neighbors of twenty years asked me over for an evening of dinner and movie-watching. They were trying to help, and in their opinion if I would start to get out, I would get back to normal more quickly. These neighbors have been so generous in my time of need, I just didn't have the heart to say no. What is really strange is that when she asked me, I knew I didn't want to go, but I thought I could do it. By that night I was a basket case. I should have called and canceled. When I arrived, they had made the same appetizers that my husband and I used to treat them to. My heart went into my stomach. I know they thought this was a kind gesture, but I just wanted to collapse. The dinner they served was my husband's favorite. I couldn't stay for the movie. My heart was beating so loud I thought they could hear it! When they asked me I should have just said no, not yet."

Breathe. Take ten deep breaths. You need to get oxygen into your system. Sit up straight, inhale through your nose with your mouth closed and then exhale through your mouth. The idea is to try to make your exhalation twice as long as your inhalation.

Stretch your shoulders and neck muscles. Relieve tension in your shoulders by shrugging them. Push shoulders up towards your ears and tighten the muscles as much as you can and then drop the shoulders and relax.

If you become familiar with the symptoms and take note when they happen, you can help yourself by trying some of the mentioned stress helpers. Please keep in mind, you didn't cause this, so don't go blaming yourself and don't treat yourself to a pity party. These symptoms are reactions to stress. They are caused by chemical changes in your brain.

It is hard to believe that a little tiny thing about the size of a grape can give you so much distress. That grape is your hypothalamus. It is located in the center of your brain. The hypothalamus stores hormones; it is responsible for temperature regulation and controls the pituitary gland. Basically this grape is the boss over your endocrine system. This is made up of glands that are ductless and release their secretions directly into the bloodstream. So this grape-sized hypothalamus is the ultimate link between your mind and your body. So when you are feeling under stress, your hypothalamus is responding in kind.

When I was in college I received the Holmes Stress Scale in Psychology 101. I have been carrying it around ever since then. Psychiatrist Dr. Thomas H. Holmes created what he called his Social Readjustment Rating Scale. This scale measures the relative stress brought on by various changes in a person's life.

The scale gives numerical values to many different types of stressful situations. Dr. Holmes was able to correlate the number of stress points a person accumulated in any two-year period with the degree of seriousness of the disorder which that person was then likely to suffer. If you accumulated more than two hundred and fifty points within a two-year period of time, you would likely be affected by a life-threatening illness. One hundred and fifty points and you might be affected by a serious illness, and fifty or less points and you might be affected with colds and flus. His scale assigned death of a spouse one hundred points. Christmas was assigned twelve points. Even simply changing your eating habits racks up fifteen points! There is stress everywhere, every day.

Overall, you are at the greatest danger for extreme stress when you lose a loved one, are exposed to extreme violence or destruction, have a loss of valued possessions, have loss of communication with loved ones, or are under intense emotional and/or physical demands.

Sometimes severe stress leads to post-traumatic stress disorder, referred to as PTSD. In this disorder you may feel like you are in a dream and you have periods of time you can not remember. Nightmares and flashbacks haunt you, and you feel like you are running on empty. You may experience panic attacks, rage, and paralyzing worry. Severe depression may set in, causing loss of hope and self-worth.

You can't escape from what has happened, but you can arm yourself for coping with stress by knowing yourself. You can anticipate stressful situations, keep a checklist of symptoms, and take an active part in relieving your stress.

In the next chapter we will go further in depression, anger and panic.

Chapter 5

Depression, Anger, and Panic

"Happiest of all mortals is he
Whose quiet mind, from vain desires is free;
Whom neither hopes, deceive, nor fears torment,
But lives at peace, within himself, content."
—George Granville

Oh happy day, contentment, peace of mind, what a wonderful state of being. I need to get me some of that! Sadly, for many people it is hard to attain. When grief saddles you up and takes you for a wild ride, you may readily weave in and out of bouts of depression, panic attacks and spurts of anger. In the last chapter, you could see how stress starts a domino effect on your physical and mental well-being. When enough dominoes fall, it may trigger one of these disturbances.

For some people depression may be depicted like the following: *Here it is, another day in a wasted life. I look into other people's eyes desperately trying to find a hint of who they really are. But I can't tell if they are like me or not. I can't let anyone really know me. I can't share my real feelings with anyone for fear that if I do, then all this will become real and I will no longer be able to pretend it isn't. When I look into the mirror I am afraid that I will see the monster that lies beneath my surface. I am too afraid. Is there anyone out there like me?* Have you ever felt this way? While walking from your car to the grocery store you pass different types of people. Do you think any of them feel this way? The news is "yes," more people than you would suspect feel this way at least once in their life.

Interviewee #46: "After my mother's death, my husband and I were having communication difficulties. We were seeing our church minister. Lucky for us he was also a psychologist. My husband was trying to fix me as I was trying to fix him. During this exploration of our relationship, I started having panic attacks. I told our minister that while lunching with a friend, I had experienced a sensation of being out of control and yet I could sense myself smiling and carrying on a conversation. My minister actually chuckled while he explained to me that no, that is not what was happening."

Unfortunately, for many years this women didn't open up to anyone else for fear of being ridiculed or not taken seriously. She was in an ocean of depression and hurt. If only he had taken her grief sincerely and realized that the circumstances in her marriage were compounding her grieving pain. Just because she could put a smile on her face and look ready to take on the day did not mean she was emotionally and physically equipped. She is one of those people that spun into an actress in order to harmonize with others. When she decided to show her real self, she was disparaged.

Even though this chapter is dealing with three feelings, you don't have to be depressed to have a panic attack. You don't have to be angry to be depressed, but more often than not these feelings are linked together in your grief.

To start taking control of your depression, you need to understand two things: depression is not a personal weakness and it is treatable. Depression affects you socially, physically, and spiritually. Socially you may not feel like you are able to interact with family and friends. You may behave rashly, cry for no reason, be irritable and angry. This behavior may plunge you into isolation. Physically you may become ill, have insomnia and fatigue. Spiritually you might have lost hope and be filled with negative thoughts as your spirit collapses.

Depression defined is an emotional state in which there are extreme feelings of sadness, dejection, lack of worth, and emptiness. Depression can be sadness coupled with a lack of energy or can grow into a chronic depression, and worse to a major depression. Chronic (persistent) depression is when you have feelings of gloom plus a change in energy, appetite and sleep habits over a two-year period of time. People with chronic depression may experience episodes of major depression. Major depression is more severe, including a loss of interest or pleasure in normal activities. Major depression interferes with everyday life. You may even think of suicide if life is perceived to not be worth living.

Loss is a common denominator in depression. Depression is more prevalent among women than men. When you have an emotional loss, it is normal to feel sadness. Many people will cope with these losses without becoming depressed. However, according to research, more than nineteen million adults suffer from clinical depression (clinical being observed and noted by a professional). If the feelings and symptoms of depression continue for a period of time, you should definitely talk with your doctor.

Just as our grief is different from anyone else's, depression also varies between individuals. The following are symptoms you may experience with depression:

Interruption of sleep habits: sleeping too much or too little
Appetite changes: overeating or loss of appetite
Indifference: loss of interest in activities that once gave you satisfaction
Irritability: uneasiness
Bodily distress: aches and pains that don't respond to treatment
Constant fatigue: feeling your energy draining out of you
Confusion: difficulty concentrating, trouble making decisions, trouble remembering
Depressed mood: persistent gloominess

If you exhibit five or more of these symptoms for longer than two weeks or if any of these symptoms interfere with getting through your daily routine, call your doctor. Remember that depression is one of the most treatable medical illnesses and it is not your fault. Please do not feel embarrassed to talk to your doctor or a qualified mental health professional.

There are genetic factors that can trigger depression.

It appears that a tendency toward depression is often genetic, but that stressful life circumstances such as a death of a loved one play a major role in bringing on depressive episodes. Chemical imbalances of natural substances in the brain allow brain cells to communicate with each other, causing biological changes that bring on depression. Life stresses and serious illness can bring on depression. Most people don't read the little warning labels on their medications. Lots of medications may cause depression, such as pain relievers, cholesterol-lowering drugs, high blood pressure medications, heart problem medications, and thyroid medications.

Interviewee #328: "My mother and father were married fifty years. My father was dying from heart failure. I noticed my mother becoming thinner and more frail. She was eating very little and drinking alcohol more. Once my father died, she seemed to stop eating all together. The doctor said she was frail but there wasn't much else wrong with her other than a broken heart. My mother died three months later from that broken heart."

I have been asked many times, can someone die from a broken heart? Yes, they can. The University of Pittsburgh looked into the fact that humans and animals can become ill and they can die from grief.

There was a study done called "The Truth About Tears." The test included 137 men and women. It is curious to think that tears help you in your depression, but they can. There are actual chemical changes that take place in the body when we cry. The tears of sadness differ in chemical makeup from the tears of joy. What is interesting about "The Truth About Tears" study is that if a grieving person talks while they cry, the emotions are contained in the words the griever speaks and not in the tears that they cry. What they found fascinating to observe was as the griever's thoughts and feelings are being spoken, the tears usually disappear. What the griever was verbalizing seemed so much more powerful than if the words had not been accompanied by tears at all.

Likewise be aware of those who cry too frequently, because they could be using the tears as a way to stop verbalizing and to stop feeling rather than to experience the emotion. The tears become a distraction from the real pain caused by the loss. So, now we know you can make good use of tears. Don't hold back, help yourself with tears.

By putting yourself in the company of nonjudgmental people, it should be safe for you to express your feelings and your tears. Tears plainly show that you are realizing the loss and allowing yourself to encounter the pain. Tears are a source of precious relief.

People say to me, "If I start to cry, I'm scared I may not be able to stop." I say to them, "If you don't start allowing your tears to flow, how will you know they won't stop?"

There is a series of studies being done on patients with major depression. These research studies have established there is a doubling of the mortality rate at any age when people suffer with major depression and do absolutely nothing about it. These studies also showed that there is relative risk for significant coronary artery disease. This research is being done to increase understanding of the underlying mechanisms to enhance the researcher's capability to predict who with major depression is most likely to develop premature heart disease, to determine the age of this susceptibility, and to develop improved means for treatment and prevention. Depression also may be a major factor in the developing of osteoporosis. Depression may cause elevated stress hormone levels, which contribute to bone loss. Other studies being done on major depression suggest that fifty to seventy percent of people are predisposed to depression by their genes. So, people with depression seem to have relatives with depression. Once again, depression is not your fault, and you are not alone.

As with all other aspects of your grief, the more you know and understand about what is going on with you, the better you can cope with it and help yourself. Depression can't really be cured, but it can be managed and overcome. Here are some suggestions for taking an active role in your depression:

– Get a physical exam to rule out any other illnesses.

– Don't oversleep. If you stay in bed for more than eight hours, you may be increasing your depressed feelings.

– If you consume alcohol, limit it. No more than one glass of wine or one beer a day.

– Healing always starts with "how" rather than "why." So ask yourself and others "How do I?" rather than "Why did this happen to me?"

– Take a walk, preferably when the sun is shining.

– Eat right. Eating omega-3 fatty acids will help.

– Try to keep communication going with family and friends. That doesn't mean you need to have long conversations—just stay in touch. One interviewee told me he didn't feel like talking and really just wanted to be left alone. A friend saw a book on the table and asked if he could read it. The friend opened the book to the spot book marked, sat down and started to read aloud. The interviewee said that he appreciated hearing another voice without having a conversation in which he would have to agree, disagree, defend, or fake.

– Prioritize

– Get support (through sharing with others in a nonjudgmental way or by reading material connected to the way you feel) and/or professional help.

– Take one day at a time. Sometimes one hour at a time. Be easy on yourself.

It is not a blemish on your character that you are depressed. We know that depression can be managed and professionally treated. Like depression, anger can also be managed.

It is normal to get angry. Stubbing your toe can make you angry, so think about what the jumbled stinging plight of grief can bring out in you!

Even though you may be angry that life has changed and the change was out of your control, you can not inflict this anger on others or direct it inwardly towards yourself. It will destroy your relationships and you. You know how stress and depression can make you feel. Anger can be felt in headaches, tight neck and shoulder muscles, a knotted stomach, tense jaw, clenched fists, your body temperature going hot or cold, and your heart races. You can't keep choking down your anger, but you can't blow up either. Try to catch your anger before it gets to that explosive point.

When you are filled with anger, you are also dealing with fear, hurt, guilt, and confusion. Sometimes you hang on to anger because it covers up the fear, the hurt, the guilt and the confusion. You can use anger to block out the reality of the death. Anger also is an adrenaline high and can make you feel like you are in control.

Interviewee #600: "My brother was killed. My dad was so mad. He just started yelling and cussing out the doctors at the hospital. He blamed everybody for my brother's death. Every day he was going to the accident scene. He was measuring things and taking pictures. I needed him to be with me. I felt like he was mad at me because I was alive and my brother was dead. When I would ask him to talk to me, he would just say he was busy working on getting justice for my brother's death."

This dad was lost in his grief and filled with his anger. He was turning his anger outward towards others, unfortunately including his daughter. He was going to show everybody he was right and he was in control.

There is also inner anger, where you become your own victim. You start thinking no one cares. Why should they? You are always wrong about everything anyway. Then there is the denial of anger. You feel numb and shut down. Some people just can't deal with what is making them angry. They just run away and hide in their work or in their solitude.

You need to be aware of the way in which you show your anger. Be honest with the people around you. Let them know what is going on with you and that you are trying hard not to inject your pain onto them. Be aware that the wrath you feel can build up. It can start as a minor irritation. Then you become more frustrated with the situation. You probably have experienced that feeling—the one where you can feel the anger swelling up inside you and all the while you are trying to get a hold of yourself. That is when you will explode and the fury will gush out like lava out of a volcano!

Anger, like grief, is one of the most misunderstood emotions. The trick to it is to acknowledge your anger. Once you do that, you can start to put your anger into a manageable outlook. As if that wasn't enough, you must also realize you are really dealing with more than anger here. You feel powerless, out of control, and guilty for what has happened. The anger may be covering up the fact that you are fearful you won't be able to cope with the loss. Keep plodding forward, because the more you understand about your anger, the less reason you will have to be afraid of your feelings.

As with your grief, you have to surrender to your anger. You must let go of grasping for control of others or of circumstances. Just concentrate on controlling yourself. You will need to find ways to safely process your anger. You can process your anger four ways: physically, emotionally, intellectually and spiritually.

Physically we can hit our bed pillows, go to the driving range and hit golf balls—my favorite is to go to the tennis court and hit with someone or against the backboard. Yard work, cleaning house, and playing a musical instrument are all good outlets.

Emotionally you can cry, yell, scream. An interviewee told me she loved going to football games so she could scream until she was limp.

Intellectually, you can write about your anger. Jot down when you first started to feel that anger hairball building up in your throat. Try to figure out what specifically caused you to start feeling that way and then try to figure out at whom the anger is really aimed.

Spiritually, spend time uplifting your spirit. For some that is reading the Bible, for others it is meditating, being out with nature, and praying.

If you are angry and have feelings of guilt, try talking to some one else about what happened and let them review it for you. Try to look at your whole relationship with your loved one. No relationship is all good or all bad. Focus on the good features and times of that relationship. Try to see what you did right rather than wrong.

Writing a letter to your loved one expressing any regrets is helpful. Write it and then put the letter away for a week. Get the letter out and reread it. See how that makes you feel. Do something positive to remember your loved one and think about how your loved one would respond to what you are doing.

Own up to your anger. Investigate what is triggering your anger and then choose a positive outlet (suggestions already mentioned in this chapter) to release your anger.

From anger let's move to panic attacks. A panic attack can happen anytime and anywhere. If you have ever had one, you won't mistake it for being ill at ease! Your heart palpitates, you have shortness of breath, you hyperventilate, you feel dizzy, your face flushes, and you may experience sweating, nausea, tightness in your throat, chest pain, and a feeling of doom. Many people feel like they are going to die. It can begin abruptly and peak within ten minutes and can last for half an hour. But like grief, everyone's panic attack differs. Some attacks may last hours and even up to a day. The panic attack is actually when intense fear prompts physical reactions in your body. Remember the fight or flight syndrome?

Just recently, panic attacks have been recognized as a condition. Also it is not unusual for panic attacks to occur together with depression.

Attacks were always just passed off as a case of nerves or it certainly just must be all in your head. Between ten and twenty percent of Americans experience panic attacks at some time in their lives. As with depression, women are more likely to have this condition than men. No one really knows what causes these attacks. It could be your genes, stress, depression, or biochemical factors, but chances are if you have a family member who has had panic attacks, your probability of having attacks is greater.

What can you do about panic attacks?

– If there are people around, talk to them—try to steady yourself.

– Take a giant yawn and breathe.

– Learn how to relax—keep telling yourself you know this will pass and you will be alright.

– Focus in on something or someone that gives you pleasure.

– Count backwards from fifty and breathe.

– Breathe deeply into a bag.

– Steady your eyes on a concrete object.

– Visualize a waterfall or a beautiful aquarium filled with

colorful fish and coral.

– In a reclined position, concentrate on one area of your body at a time and relax it. For example, start with your foot. Concentrate on feeling your foot completely give in and relax, then move to your calf.

– Tighten the muscles in one area of your body and hold for the count of twenty and then move on to the next area.

– Know that the attack will end.

"I woke up in the middle of the night. I needed to go to the bathroom. I felt sort of giddy. When I got up, my legs were like rubber. I fell to the floor. For the first time in my life, my legs failed me. On top of that, the room started spinning. I could not believe it. I kept trying to get up. Finally my husband heard me and got out of bed to help. I noticed that I had been experiencing facial tics and that I had trouble getting my breath, but I didn't think much about it other than it was uncomfortable. My heart started beating so fast and so loud I thought other people could hear it. Then I felt like I couldn't swallow. My throat felt like it was closing up and I couldn't catch my breath. My husband picked me up and dashed me off to the nearest doctor. When I was at the doctor's office, I don't know why but I felt like 'I just can't be here.' The doctor didn't come fast enough, and I was scared. I hobbled out of the waiting room to find my husband. I just wanted out of there. He took me to another doctor, letting them know they had to see me now." (Interviewee #715)

There are three kinds of panic attacks. There are the unexpected ones. The attack just comes out of nowhere without any kind of warning. Then there are the ones brought on by specific situations that always cause panic for you, such as being in a closed-off small room or having to sit in the very back of a large airplane. The third would be a situation in which you are likely to have a panic attack but it doesn't always happen.

When you suffer from panic attacks, it can be very frustrating and terrifying for your family and friends. If possible you need to talk with them and ask for their understanding; after all, they may have experienced this, too.

Panic attacks, like depression, are not your fault. There is no reason to be embarrassed or to blame yourself.

Depression, panic, and anger may all be part of your grief. You experience much of this because the pain of letting go of your loved one is intense. Don't be intimidated by your emotions. Trust that when you feel you need help, you *do*—and seek it out. Let people around you know it is hard enough to get through your grief; you don't need to feel like an outcast, too. The only person that can strip you of your dignity is you.

Chapter 6

Are They Hallucinations or For Real?

"...I'm getting closer, but I don't know what to."
—Dan Fogelberg: *I'm Missing You*

"I sank into a status of numbness of all my physical sensory tools, so nearly into the status of dying. But my inner life and thinking remained, so that I was able to perceive and keep in memory those things, which happened there and how they happen to those who are awakened from the dead ... Especially I was aware of that there was a pulling and dragging of the mind, the same of my soul, out of my body."
—Emanuel Swedenborg (1688-1772)

There had been a funeral. On the way home from the funeral an accident happened. I was knocked out—I mean really knocked out. What I remember is walking through a meadow. It was filled with huge, brilliant-colored flowers—colors like I had never seen before and I have never been able to describe accurately. Filled with such happiness and peace, I walked towards a river of sparkling, golden, flowing water. A bridge appeared from the meadow to the other side, where I saw Jesus and my relatives that were no longer confined to this earth. I impatiently felt myself wanting to cross the bridge, and then the bridge disappeared. I was denied entry. I was told Jesus died for us and the accident was not supposed to happen—it was not my time. I was told I was not finished yet; there were things to do. I was then told that since no one would want to believe me, there would be certain things to look for so I would know this happened. One was even though the car was demolished, my glasses would be found and be wearable until I could get a new pair. I was also told the ribbon taken off flowers at the funeral would still be in the trunk unmarred. One last thing was we, in the accident, would be fine.

Then all of a sudden I felt myself high in the sky. I didn't feel like I was alone, looking down at this poor creature laying on the side of the highway. People were all around being upset and looking at the small person. The incredible overwhelming compassion I felt for this life laying on the side of the road is so profound there is no way I can explain it. All of a sudden I felt yanked from the sky and pulled into that body laying by the side of the road. I entered through the head. The next thing I remember is people shouting at me to wake up. When I woke I was excited to tell my story. The looks on their faces!! No one liked it and no one wanted it repeated.

That happened more than thirty years ago and I can recall it as if it happened yesterday. It no longer matters to me if anyone else thinks it was real. It is real to me. For many years I would not talk about this and still have been very careful as to whom I would share this with. Now, here it is for anyone who cares to read about it. So that you know, my glasses were found where I was told they would be found, the ribbon was where it was supposed to be, and there were no lasting problems from this accident where the car went side over side—some even say end over end—and was crushed.

I had two problems with this "vision." One was for many years I thought I must be insane or I was the only one to have this happen. Can you imagine how arrogant that thinking was? But no one would talk about these kind of things for fear of humiliation, so I didn't realize I was one of many. The other problem was I kept thinking what was I supposed to accomplish with my life. What was my calling? Finally one day I woke up and had the answer. It was simply to be kind to others. It was to smile at others when you don't feel like it. Hold the door open for the next person. You never know when a person is going through a desperate time and they see a warm smile and a kind gesture and that makes a difference to them. It's the little things that can make the biggest changes.

The word "hallucination" comes from the Latin word "*alucinari*," meaning to wander in mind. It was first introduced to psychiatric literature by Esquirol in 1837. Hallucinations have long been connected to mental illness. That is one reason people are so afraid to talk about what they think they—or actually do—feel, see, hear, and/or smell. Hallucinations are defined as something sensed that is not caused by an outside event. It could be something heard, seen, smelled or felt. Hallucinations can be a symptom of many different diseases and conditions. They can be a result of the brain metabolism being altered from its normal level. A high fever could affect your brain metabolism. Withdrawal from medications or drugs can also cause hallucinations by affecting your brain metabolism. Sensory and sleep deprivation have also accounted for hallucinations.

We have all heard the stories of the drunk seeing the pink elephant, the person drying out from drugs believing bugs are crawling under his skin, the person who lost their hearing hearing music, or the amputee still feeling the leg that was cut off.

People experiencing hallucinations at any age are suspected to have a medical or a neurological disease. If you are elderly, then it must be dementia; surely it couldn't be acceptable to think it just might be real.

There is a syndrome called the Charles Bonnet Syndrome which is characterized by episodes of visual hallucinations in the elderly. This syndrome probably stems from many underlying causes, including insufficient blood supply to the brain.

Some researchers acknowledge the difference between hallucinations and delusions. We already defined hallucinations. Delusions are defined as a false idea—a misinterpretation of a situation. An example of a delusion would be thinking everybody at a party is talking about you. With the hallucination you can see, feel, hear, smell, and taste something that isn't really there. Or can you?

Researchers Bill and Judy Guggenheim coined a phrase: "after-death communication experiences." They called this ADC for short. They say that what they considered to be real communication has been explained away as grief-induced hallucinations brought on by wishful thinking or need. They also acknowledge that ADC could happen to a person before he or she even knew about the death of a loved one. People who are having ADCs report seeing the deceased, hearing them, smelling them, and sometimes even being touched by them. Other researchers recognize death-bed visions. The person dying reports seeing angels, deceased loved ones, Jesus and other religious figures, sometimes hours to days before they die.

Dr. Melvin Morse, M.D., an Associate Professor of Pediatrics at the University of Washington, has studied near-death experiences in children for fifteen years. He tells of a young girl who had no heartbeat for nineteen minutes. When she recovered she told him the details of being taken down a "brick-lined tunnel to a heavenly place."

In 1975, Dr. Raymond A. Moody's bestselling book *Life After Life* brought attention to near-death experiences. Dr. Moody's research included one hundred and fifty people who died or almost died, recovered and told of their vision. Dr. Moody has defined nine elements that may transpire during the near-death experience: hearing a buzzing or ringing noise; having an overall feeling of peace with no pain; feeling like one is out of one's body; going through a tunnel at high speed; seeing the earth from the heavens; seeing people from the other side with an inner light; meeting a spiritual being such as God, Jesus or an angel; reliving every act one has ever done to other people, bringing one to the realization that love is life; and a reluctance to return back to one's body. Not all people who have been close to death report having near-death experiences. About thirty-five percent report having one, while sixty-five percent say they do not.

Near-death experiences usually show a high brain activity. This activity means the near-death experience is the same as it is assumed for dreams. There is a lot of research going on with near-death experiences. Scientist are searching for circumstances under which these visions might be artificially induced. Some scientist simply want to prove that these visions are neurobiological functions. Because of this, so many people are still hesitant to come forward or to discuss these experiences with their doctors. Even though so many people do not want to come forward or even talk with their doctors about these experiences for fear they will be labeled "loony," about eight hundred million people in the U.S. claim to have had this type of vision.

The Bible is filled with reports of miracles and appearances. Also noted is that Pope Gregor the Great collected reports of these experiences and asked the respected persons on his own. His reports included a soldier's description: "He said there was a bridge, under which flew a black, dark stream evaporating a fog with unbearable stench. Above the bridge were friendly, green meadows, decorated with pleasant-smelling flower arrangements on which white-dressed humans seemed to stand together. Such fragrance prevailed on that location, so that even there strollers and living were totally fulfilled. There everyone had his home brightened by wonderful light."

Since the early 1900's, researchers have been trying to connect the dots to make sense of these types of hallucinations. One of the most outstanding reports showed that some people on their death beds had visions of people coming for them that they didn't even know had already died.

Interviewee #72: "Who is my mother talking to? Could this be real? My mom came to live with us when she could no longer take care of herself. The doctor was saying it would just be a matter of time. One night I couldn't sleep, so I got up to lay on the couch in the living room. The room we had set up for her was on the other side of the living room. I could hear her talking. She was actually having a conversation. She was talking to her brother, my dad, her sister, and her mother. They are all dead. She was talking to them like they were sitting all around her. I went in and asked her if she knew she was talking out loud. She said, 'Can't you see them?' I was scared to death. She then told me that my deceased relatives had been coming for several nights now. They were telling her she would be joining them soon. I don't know what to believe. Part of me thinks this was really real and another says that it must be the pain medication. Whatever it was, it made her feel more comfortable."

Death bed visions are described as paranormal experiences of the dying. These visions are significant because they provide evidence in support of survival of consciousness after death. Not that this evidence is scientific. These visions seem to share certain traits. The dying person feels profound peace and elation. James Hyslop and E. Bozzano, psychical researchers, collected and studied cases of death-bed visions around the turn of the twentieth century. The first systematic study was done in 1924 by Sir William Barret, an English professor of physics and a psychical researcher. His wife piqued his interest when she, a physician specializing in obstetrical surgery, told him about one of her patients who had a death-bed vision right before he died. Further study into death-bed visions by researchers Karlis Osis and Erlendur Haraoldsson showed that the patients having these visions were fully conscious.

Interviewee #89: "Well, I'm not gonna die today, but it's close. Every day I see the chariot and the horses in the upper left-hand corner of my room. Jesus says it will be soon—get ready."

This woman died three days after her first vision. Her family said that it must have been the pain medication. Is it true or not? The dying woman was at peace and was reassured by her vision. Does it matter if someone else believes it?

Interviewee #54: "I was abruptly awakened. I was more curious than afraid about what I saw. I saw two bright yellow orbs floating in the air. One was brighter and larger than the other. I heard my deceased husband talking to me. I sat up in bed staring at the floating balls of light. He was letting me know he was okay and there was an afterlife. He needed to go and not come back anymore. I needed to let him go. I believe this happened, and I have not seen anything like that again. I tried telling a few people and was not successful in getting them to accept this. I don't drink, and I wasn't taking any kind of medication. I know what I saw and I know what I heard."

Interviewee # 12: "When I answered the phone, at first I didn't hear anyone. Then I heard a voice. It was my son. All he said was 'I love you, Mom,' and then the phone went dead. This was very unusual because my son was in another state on a business trip and we mostly talked once a week on Sundays. Later on I found out that my son had been in a car accident on his way to his business meeting and was in a deep coma. When I received the call he had already been in a coma for four and half hours."

Interviewee # 375: "I was driving on the expressway. I was going through a very bad time in my life. I was contemplating thoughts of suicide and how I could make it look like an accident by just driving into a tree. All of sudden I smelled my grandfather. He always had this smell to him like fresh baked bread. From the time I was little, I loved cuddling up with him. I always felt secure. The smell became stronger, so I started talking to him and asked for help. All I know is my thinking started becoming calmer, and my believing he is near me is helping me turn my life around."

Interviewee # 442: "My husband and I lost our only children to an accident. Our son was driving with our daughter in the passenger seat. A truck ran a red light and smashed into them. The doctors say they didn't know what hit them. Our son was killed instantly; our daughter lived for eleven days without ever regaining consciousness. When my husband and I started going through some of their things, we found an essay written by my daughter for her eighth grade class. This essay was written three months before her death. In it she wrote how little time people really have on this earth. She continued, saying that God allows parents to have some children only for a little while and that parents should be appreciative rather than sad if they should lose their children. She wrote about angels being all around and that you just have to listen closely to hear them. My husband and I feel that my daughter must have known her life would be cut short."

Hallucinations or truth? It is all in how you choose to believe it.

Chapter 7

Fables and Lies

"It is only with the heart that one can see rightly; what is essential is invisible to the eye."
—Antoine De Saint-Exupery

"My friends are telling me I should be out dating. My husband has been dead one year this month. I don't feel like I am mentally ready for dating. I'm still just getting used to my life. They say I should be over my husband." (Interviewee #59)

If you have lost a loved one, I am sure you have heard someone use these phrases: "You will get over this," and, "...when things get back to normal." People have good intentions, but mostly they are set on getting everybody back into a comfort zone. Since well-meaning people don't know how to really help you, they try to rescue you from your grief. What they don't realize is that the more they try to rescue you, the more you feel knots of despair. Well-intentioned people want to dry up your tears, get you out to a movie, pack up your loved one's belongings, and get you back to normal as soon as possible. Well-intentioned people come equipped with a snoot full of "should and must." It is not like we don't already "should" ourselves to death. We don't need others jumping on that bandwagon.

There is no need to put a bumper sticker on the back of your car that says "grieving person on board," but you do need some nonjudgmental understanding.

As we have already discussed, you need to take an active part in your grief in order to get to the other side of your new reality. If you have ever wanted to attain a goal or had to get through any kind of addiction problem, medical situation, or another type of personal or business loss, then you had to take action. You planned, thought, gathered information, found people who could help, and kept plugging towards your goal every day. Getting through your grief is no different.

Others don't seem to realize this fact. Sometimes others just say the dumbest, most bizarre things, thinking they will help. The following are some of the fables and lies that I hear most about grief:

Fable 1. "You should be over this by now." Who says? I don't know why people want to ramrod this kind of thinking down anyone's throat. The person saying this has no idea of your grief, and they are unaware of the variables that make your grief different. Tell this person they need to get over you not being over it yet!

Fable 2. "Your aches and pains are all in your head." The doctors may not find a broken bone, but the medical field is well aware of what stress and depression can do to your body. You are not crazy—you're stressed in your grief.

Fable 3. "You need to go through all the grieving "stages" one by one." As we discussed in the chapter on mazes, stages, and phases, you may experience some or all of those emotions. It depends on your variables along with your stress level and the loss you are experiencing.

Fable 4. "I have been exactly in your shoes and I know how you feel." No one has walked in your shoes, and if they did, they would walk in them differently. They may have had a similar experience and their heart may be filled with compassion for you, but they are not you—their loved one was not your loved one. It is different.

Fable 5. "You should get out more." You will, when you are ready. Now if you can't get out of your bathrobe and it has been a while since you showered, you need to get out to go to your doctor.

Fable 6. "Time will take care of this." How many times have we all been told time takes care of everything! Grief is like an inert mass until you start to participate and get some control of what is happening. Time will not take care of "this"; the effort you put forth during the time is what is important.

Fable 7. "They were so ill, this couldn't have been a surprise to you." This one is my personal pet peeve. Yes, many times the person was ill for months, maybe even years. That is the point. You were told that any day now your loved one will die. Several days come and go and no death. So you start to get used to the idea of the loved one still being here. Then one day, all of a sudden, they are not. Did you know they were going to die?—yes. Did you know exactly when?—no. Was it a surprise it actually happened?—yes. Does your life change?—yes.

Fable 8. "It's God's way." Sometimes it may not seem like an act of God to take your loved one. When your person is taken from this life suddenly from a crime, accident, sudden heart attack, you have trouble making sense of all this. Think of looking at a picture of a puppy. Everyone looking at that same picture will interpret what they see the same way, even if we think the meaning behind the picture is different. We connect the dots in our minds to see the same picture so it makes sense. When a sudden death happens, we keep trying to connect the dots to get this to make some kind of sense so we can accept it. We end up not ever being able to connects those dots.

Interviewee #27: "I don't understand why God would let this happen. I feel like I have lost all faith. Why not take me? My daughter was 32 years old. She had a wonderful husband and two small children. Now they are motherless. Why did she have to get cancer?"

This mother eventually worked through her anger and found her faith again. Many people for the first time will go to God, while others may turn away with anger for a while.

Fable 9. "Get rid of the deceased's possessions right away." I have had people tell me how they have regretted well-meaning friends and family coming into the home and collecting clothes, doing wash, even taking down pictures.

Interviewee #743: "I felt so lost after my mother died. She was supposed to meet us for dinner. My aunt was going to pick my mother up and meet us at the restaurant. I talked to my mother just a few hours before she was to meet us. Everything was fine. My aunt went to pick her up and mother didn't answer the door. She was gone from a heart attack. When we first went into her house after her death, I asked for people to leave everything where it was. I went into the bedroom. I took my mother's nightgown and her pillow case. They both still smelled of her. When we got home I put her pillowcase on my pillow. Some of my relatives thought I was nuts. I can't tell you the comfort that gave me. I am grateful everyone allowed me to take my time in organizing and getting rid of most items. By doing it my way, I believed it helped me with my grief."

Fable 10. "If you cry too much, people will think you're losing control." There is no doubt you are in a fragile state. Tears, for some people, occur when they experience sadness as well as magnificence. Many of us get misty hearing our National Anthem. Tears can merge delight and sorrow. You may be a person more easily hurt than most or more tense than most.

Fable 11. "They are no longer in pain; you should be grateful." We are never ready to have a loved one no longer on this physical plane. We may feel a relief for our loved one being out of pain, but that doesn't mean we feel relief for ourselves.

Fable 12. "You should move right away." You shouldn't make any big decisions right away. Realize that whenever you make a decision, you are choosing one thing over another. If you are overwhelmed in your grief, if may be hard to be certain of what you would least mind sacrificing.

Fable 13. "You shouldn't change what you normally do." Everything has changed. The second the death happened, life changed. The whole grief course is the process of moving from how life used to be to how it is now.

Fable 14. "Men and women grieve the same way." Knowing that the variables that make our life different from everyone else's, this statement is not true.

Fable 15. "Death is the only kind of loss you grieve." Absolutely not! There are many kinds of emotional losses. They can range from divorce, to loss of family communication, to loss of a dream.

Fable 16. "Everybody in grief goes through the same things."

We know that is far from the truth. No one is exactly like you, no one had the same relationship as you had with your loved one, no one has the exact same financial conditions or physical conditions you do.

Fable 17. "You must be over it; you look good." Many people in grief seem to separate into two selves—one they put out to the world and the other they keep hidden. Remember, grief is the best acting teacher around!

Fable 18. "You must be over it; you're laughing a lot." People deal with their grief in many different ways. Laughing is good. It is a wonderful release and a pleasing memory that usually makes us laugh. You also know that your loved one would want you to laugh and enjoy the memories. Laughter brings us together and breaks down barriers, making it easier to talk with one another. Don't make the mistake of not laughing because you think it is demeaning to your loved one.

Fable 19. "You shouldn't talk about your loss so much." Talking and sharing about your loved one is essential to your grief work.

Fable 20. "You will forget about your loved one." Never. Love doesn't die. Your loved one is always with you in your heart and in your memories. If you lost a spouse and you find a new love, you don't forget—you get a new viewpoint.

Fable 21. "How long you are committed to your grief defines your love for the deceased."

> Interviewee #97: "It has been over a year and I feel guilty if I get happy for anything. I feel ashamed if I start to have a good time."

Make sure you are not building a new relationship—with your pain. Sometimes people get so attached to their pain they forget to live their life. How long you grieve does not prove or disprove the depth of your love.

As far as the lies, those come from you—the griever. When you are acting a certain way that is different from the way you feel, you are fibbing up a storm! When someone asks you if you need help and you say "no" because you don't want to seem weak, that's a whopper. If neighbors or co-workers ask how you are doing and you answer "fine, thank you," I bet you just shuffled around the truth.

Learn how to answer truthfully. If someone asks if you would like to go to a movie, and you are not sure, answer him or her like this: "Right now I feel like I might want to go, but I am not sure if I will be up to it later. If it is okay that I can give you short notice as to whether I will go or not, then I'll let you know later." Let people know "today is not a good day, but I appreciate you asking," or "right this moment I feel fine; thanks for asking." How can you expect people to learn what to say to you or how to help you if you don't come clean with them?

Chapter 8

Exercise in Truth

"To most of us nothing is so invisible as an unpleasant truth. Though it is held before our eyes, pushed under our noses, rammed down our throats—we know it not."

—Eric Hoffer

Today your world may be great; tomorrow your world may seem like nothing is going right. Today you may be sick and tired of being sick and tired, and yet when someone asks you how you are doing, you will tell them you are doing just fine.

When you decide to take on an exercise in truth, it will require courage and integrity. Facing the truth about your grief can make you fearful. The fear may put pressure on you to face up to what you really are feeling.

Some people like to write down their feelings. Others like to think privately, and others like to talk into a tape recorder and replay it and then erase it.

When you are knee-deep in grief, it seems like a herculean task to get on with life. Any time anything in your life changes, it usually isn't easy. Being the creatures of control that we are, most of us are not too pleased being confronted with transformation. It isn't easy to regulate your life with being positive when life is so unstable.

Grief can be cruel, and it violates everything we ever thought about our lives. Trying to resolve your grief is to immerse yourself in truth: The truth about the death. The truth about the relationship. The truth about your own anger. The truth about your own guilt. The truth about your new reality.

You can't let grief bring your life to a screeching halt. You have to take action. As we said before, any time you set out to conquer an illness, a goal, a family project, you have to work at it.

The first thing you do is educate yourself with the pros and the cons of what you are trying to accomplish. You determine what kind of help or tools that you need. You proceed by making a plan, and then you follow the plan until completion. Sometimes you make adjustments, so you need to remain flexible. The one factor you must attain confidence in is that you can accomplish your goal. You are the only one that really knows what you are capable of and what you are not, when you need help and when you are better off without it.

What does this have to do with getting through grief? Everything. You need to know yourself. This journey is certainly going to accomplish that, but you also have to start the journey with a combination of objectivity and subjectivity.

"It is necessary to the happiness of man that he be mentally faithful to himself. Infidelity does not consist in believing, or in disbelieving; it consists in professing to believe what he does not believe."
—Thomas Paine, Anglo-American
political theorist, writer

To start your exercise in truth, you must leave your shadow

self behind. Everything you see or hear—you either trust it or not; you either have faith in it or not.

Look inside yourself and try to answer these questions. You may feel like right now might not be the time, but sooner or later you need to take an inventory of the relationship you had with the deceased. This is strictly between you and a piece of paper. Write what you feel, not what you think.

My emotional losses in life include ?
I feel like I handled those losses how ?
How do I feel right now ?
What has been the hardest part of my grief to deal with ?
Am I listening to my intuition ?
I am angry at ?
Confrontation makes me feel ?
The last person who upset me was ?
Two things I expect most from my family are ?
I believe death is ?
If I had it to do all over again I would change ?
I feel resentful about ?
The person who helps me the most is ?
I need ?
I wish others would treat me ?
If I could change one thing about myself, it would be ?
My attitude affects ?
I am most happy when ?
I miss my loved one most when ?
The trait I miss most about my loved one is ?
I feel guilty about ?
My loved one's favorite thing to do was ?
My favorite memory is ?
My relationship with my loved one was ?

I feel lonely when ?
Three things I like most about myself are ?
It is easy to forgive myself ?
My favorite place to go is ?
The funeral made me feel ?
I feel like I can be honest with this person ?
My favorite photograph is ?
What were the best parts of my relationship with deceased ?

Answering these questions will help you understand and attain peace of mind. By probing deeply, you will find the true foundation of your relationship. So many times, people concentrate on the end rather than the full relationship experienced with their loved one.

Interviewee #74: "The last my wife said to me was she would home for dinner. I was irritated with her for going to one more charity function. I had stopped going years ago. With three children and a full-time job, I don't know where she got her energy. Always in a hurry, she was applying her make-up while racing down the highway. I don't remember what they said about the cell phone. All I could concentrate on was the last few weeks she was alive. We had argued a lot over the charity work, the kids, and believe it or not, we were fighting over our vacation plans! Married fourteen years and all I could think about was how sorry I was for being so aggravated with her. I was actually mad at her for making me mad. I am still mad at her for driving while doing her make-up. I am still mad at her for leaving these beautiful children. I am still mad at her for breaking her promise to me that we would be together forever. It never occurred to me at our age either one of us could die. It certainly didn't cross my mind that she would be first. Even being mad, I needed to find a way to try and take the arguments back. No matter how hard I tried, I couldn't. What I would have given to talk with her one more time. When I finally put the relationship in perspective and could see the fourteen years as a whole, I realized there had been so much good. We had our ups and downs, but we loved each other. The good outweighed the bad. With help in seeing the relationship in totality, I have been able to choose what to remember and concentrate on that."

The gentleman, like so many people, was feeling regretful, angry, and guilty. Desperately fighting with yearning to turn back the clock. Concentrating on the worst, not the best, he was feeding into his nightmare. Now she can walk with him in his dreams and in his heart every day. She can bring a smile to his face from a pleasant memory. He can talk openly with his children about her. He can go on with his life knowing his love is still alive and not tainted with anguish.

Interviewee #36: "My brother committed suicide six months ago. My mother and father refuse to talk about the suicide. They insist it was an accident. Tell me how blowing off your head is an accident. I try to tell them how troubled he was. He was into drugs. My mother puts him up on a pedestal. You would think he had been a saint. My younger brother is really feeling the pressure. He is confused by their lies, and like me, he doesn't understand why they can't admit what my brother was really like."

The dynamics of a family change when a death occurs. It is said that when you lose a parent, you lose your past. When you lose a spouse, you lose your present. When you lose a child, you lose your future.

Many parents think they are protecting their children from the pain of grief. Children sometimes try to rescue their parents from the pain. This family had a lot of unresolved issues. They had complicated grief issues. These parents needed to have a laundry day with the truth. They needed to come clean with what happened. They were afraid to face up to the part they believed they played in his suicide. In talking with them, they both told how they knew about the drug use. They thought it would pass. They both noticed the boy's change in behavior. The grades dropped, he was caught skipping school, he stole from his parents, and he was isolating himself from his family. The parents were hiding the truth about the relationships they had with each other and their son. They were fearful of accepting the truth about their son's behavior. They were now swimming in an ocean of guilt. The only way they knew to deal with the guilt was to sweep it under the pedestal on which they were now putting the memory of their son.

The daughter had certain expectations of her parents. She expected them to hold the family together and face the situation head-on. She expected the family members would support each other, not hush each other up.

The youngest son was falling between the cracks. His parents believed he was not feeling any pain over his brother's death since the child would one minute show sadness and the next be laughing and ready to play. The parents didn't realize that children's grief comes and goes in spurts.

Once this family made a commitment to get beyond the loss and to help each other in their grief work, they allowed themselves to focus on the family's truth. They realized grief work takes courage, that seeing it for what it was and choosing what to take in the future takes love and hope. Talking about their grief and listening to others helped them cope.

One way you know you are healing is when you can get the thoughts out of your mind and into words. My Grief Workshops are set up for small groups. Even though it is a series, people can come at any point. I make sure the people know they do not have to participate in any way. Some people are ready to participate. Those that share have most likely healed a little more and are at a better place than some of the others. There are some people who are just naturally shy or grew up with "don't air out your dirty laundry" and they feel uncomfortable sharing. Some of them share in later meetings and some of them don't. The ones that don't share in a group setting always come up to me at the end to talk privately. And that's okay, too.

It is important that when people do participate, they feel protected and comfortable. They know their words will not boomerang on them and come back to slice further into their grief pain.

There are also workshops for children. I am one of these people who believe strongly that when children are overlooked in grief, the emotions manifest into negative acts. Children usually gauge how they should behave by the family's expectations. The 1990 U.S. Bureau of the Census said that nationwide approximately one in twenty children experience the loss of a parent before they reach the age of eighteen. You can imagine if adults have trouble understanding and dealing with grief what the children are going through.

So many children are left on their own to figure it all out. It is so confusing to them, they have trouble putting it into words. The grief can come out in physical symptoms or in negative behavior. Children, like adults, have to face their fears, their anger, their guilt, and their pain.

Children may experience loss of appetite or obsessive eating. They may have nightmares. Children may become aggressive, exhibiting bouts of eruptive behavior or self-destructive behavior. They may go on a blaming spree. Children can and do experience depression, anger, and panic. Like adults, they also have to find a way to get to the other side of their pain. They too must create a "new normal" for their life without the deceased.

You can help your children by talking with them or getting them to talk to someone. Take certain pictures and ask the child to tell you about the picture. This opens up the memory bank. Don't judge or criticize the child if you find their dreams, visions, or thoughts not to be ones you feel comfortable with. Tell them to write a letter to the deceased, and if they want to share it, listen to it with an open heart. Answer the children's questions honestly. Most children want to know what is going to happen next—"Who is going to take care of me?" Sometimes, children may be afraid that since one person has died, everyone else will die soon. Children will ask if you know when they will die. Try to maintain regular routines for the children. Assure, share, encourage, and be honest with children.

We all have "mind chatter." The "if only," the "I should have," the "I wish I hadn't," and the other flashes of anxiety. An exercise in truth will help you calm the mind and get on with living the rest of your life in harmony.

Chapter 9

Pain Relievers

"I walked a mile with Pleasure;
She chattered all the way,
But left me none the wiser
For all she had to say.
I walked a mile with Sorrow
And never a word said she;
But, oh, the things I learned from her
When Sorrow walked with me!"
                    —R.B. Hamilton

Sorrow can make you or break you. Which will it be? "Difficult" is not a descriptive enough word to represent what it is like to move ahead with life when you are in so much pain. Becoming aware of what to do about your grief is up to you once you have the knowledge as presented in this book. Continue to gather as much information as you can. Information along with understanding will knock the stumbling blocks from your path so the sorrow and pain can wane.

While grief is pounding you, don't overlook what you need to do for you. When you start thinking about tomorrow, you are experienceing a part of healing. The following are suggestions that will help:

Set goals. Start with small goals. What do you want to accomplish this hour? It may take some time for you to be able to plan for the next day or the next week. It is hard to set goals when one minute you feel fine and the next you want to get into bed, pull the covers over your head and never emerge again. Take it little by little. Eventually, you will be able to set goals for the future.

Take time for yourself. Take time alone so you can regroup and think. Take time because you tire easily with the stress. Take the time to rest—no need to be superperson.

Talk. Find that nonjudgmental person you can trust, whether it be a friend, family member, someone you find in a support group, or a professional.

When someone offers help, ask them to be specific. What are they really willing to do? Be direct when you ask for help. Picking up prescriptions, going to the grocery store, lending a hand with cleaning the house, laundry, or helping with yard work are all things that you may need and would appreciate help with.

Learn to relax. Sounds so easy, doesn't it? One way to relax is to focus on a word or a phrase that is pleasing to you. By concentrating on this word or phrase, you can block out unpleasant thoughts. You can practice this several times a day. If that is not comfortable, at least try to practice it once daily.

For some people to take a hot shower or a leisurely bath helps them to relax. Try stretching your body. Turn on music and move your body to the rhythm.

Another way of relaxing is to imagine you are inhaling up from the bottom of your feet; bring the breath up through your legs and into your stomach area. Try to feel the breath nourishing you. Then exhale, allowing the breath to flow back down through your feet.

Try this relaxation technique: lying on your back, start the relaxation process with one part of your body at a time. Start with your right foot. Acknowledge the foot, then focus on relaxing the foot. Once the foot is relaxed, move to the calf, and so on until the entire body—one area at a time—is in a relaxed mode.

You can also try to picture yourself in a pleasant place. While you are visualizing the place, allow your body to go limp. Take in deep breaths. Try this for ten minutes. If you hands are warm, chances are you are relaxed; if your hands are cold, you are most likely still tensed up.

Carry or wear something of the deceased. Even though the relationship is now one-sided, you still have your love for the person. By wearing something or keeping something tucked away near by, you can feel connected physically with your loved one.

Seek out a support group. Determine what kind of grief support group you might like to participate in or listen in on. There are support groups for specific losses, such as loss of a child, loss by violence, loss of a spouse. There are some support groups that deal with general feelings of loss. Talk to the person who is handling the support group. Ask what is expected of you. Ask if you have to participate or if you can just listen.

When friends and family ask you out, tell them to be explicit. When you have experienced a loss, some types of entertainment you liked before the death may not be funny or comforting at this point. If it is going to be a gathering of people, ask who will be there.

Take cheer in small delights. Nature is full of splendor and peacefulness. Notice when the sun is shining, notice the formation of the clouds. Take a walk or listen to your favorite music. Your loved one is tucked into your heart, so talk to your loved one and let them him or her know the magnificence of the day. Tell him or her how you yearn for him or her to be able to enjoy this with you.

Interviewee #17: "I had breakfast with my wife every morning, even after she died. We had breakfast together for forty years; why stop now? At first I use to put a plate out for her. Then I decided to just put a candle where her plate would be. I would light the candle every morning and I would tell her what I was going to do that day and that I missed her. When I was done with breakfast, I put out the flame and went on with my day. My family thought I was a brick short. They came to see that lighting that candle gave me some happiness. I told them I knew she wasn't coming back, but I believed she was watching over me. I no longer light the candle because I don't need to now. A lady friend came into my life. She knows I still love my wife, but I have room in my heart for her, too. When I brought her over to my house the first time, I did light that candle, and I introduced my new lady to my wife. I told my wife how happy this lady made me. I know my wife would want me to go on and enjoy the life I have left."

Many people have told me they continue to talk with their loved ones for years. Some people talk to pictures of the deceased. Some visit gravesides. While tiding up the ground around the grave, they talk to their deceased loved ones. One interviewee took a chair every day at lunch time and would eat her lunch and talk to her fiancé. She had felt so left out because she was the fiancée and not the wife. The fiancé's parents took over gathering his belongings, making arrangements and decisions. She was left out. Coming to the graveside helped her work out her perception of the events that took place.

Some talk to their loved ones in their dreams. When a young man of twenty-four died, his friends gathered with picnic baskets in hand. They sat around the graveside and held their own memorial to the young man by remembering their fondest memories of him. Whatever helps you, do. After all it is your grief—no one else's.

Interviewee #88: "My husband was a manager for a large company. When he died, I went to his office to pick up his personal effects. They [the company] had been very considerate and waited for me to bundle his belongings up. My husband's secretary was standing guard to jump in and help. I found a novel my husband had been reading. One of my pleasures was to bring that book home and read it myself. I felt close to him, and to tell you the truth I had no idea he had a fondness for this kind of mystery novel. I learned something about him and that made me joyful."

Listening to your loved one's music, reading a book he/she liked, eating a meal the two of you enjoyed together can all help when the time is right.

Interviewee #569: "When the radio station I was listening to would play 'our music,' it just drove me crazy. I couldn't stand it. I don't think I will ever be able to listen to certain songs again. The pain is unbearable."

Everybody is different and unique in their grief. Do what is right for you.

Many people will find a place in their yard and plant a tree, bush, or flowers dedicated to their loved one. They receive gratification from tending to the plants.

You need to permit yourself to cry. Whether you shed a few tears or weep, if you feel like doing it—do it.

You need to eat right, take your medications as prescribed, and exercise. You couldn't control the circumstances that pitched you into grief, but you can control what you do for yourself.

You need to have hope. Hope for the future. Hope knowing that all will be well. Hope to help you get through the grief work. Hope for the pain to subside and be replaced by loving memories.

You need to allow yourself to make changes. If you want to or need to get rid of things, want to rearrange the furniture, change where you sleep, it is fine. Don't second guess yourself, and it really isn't anyone else's job to second guess you.

Know that is it good to say "no." Remember those well-intentioned people who ask you to lunch, to dinner, to a movie, or to come over and help you? If you feel like it, that's great, but if you don't feel like it, don't put yourself in the position of more stress. Grief is stressful enough without stacking more pressure on your shoulders. Be honest and stand firm.

Know that it is okay to laugh and enjoy life again. When you are able to enjoy yourself and others around you, it does not in any way diminish your love or memories of your loved one.

Life is best lived one day at a time. When you feel a wave of grief ready to wash over you, stay in the moment. Concentrate on what is happening right then.

Remember your loved one by making a collage or a memory

scrapbook. Have people who knew and cared for your loved one write a few of their favorite memories.

Make a treasure box and place favorite photos and keepsakes in it. You might even take the ribbons from the funeral flowers to put into the box or perhaps make a design with them.

Take some of your loved one's clothes and make a quilt or pillows.

Make a memory frame to place your loved one's picture in. Put the word "Courage" on the top left corner to represent the grit it takes to get through your grief. In the top right corner place the word "Sorrow" to represent the pain you have suffered. In the bottom left corner place the word "Devotion" to represent the everlasting love. In the bottom right hand corner place the work "Faith" to represent the hope for the future.

Loving with all your heart is wonderful and fulfilling. When the person you love dies, it makes sense that you will grieve fiercely. It takes courage and strength to face up to your grief. It takes more bravery to ask for help than it does to go around alone with a "stiff upper lip."

Getting through your grief will reward you not only with a life to be lived in brilliance, but also with a gift. The gift of healing tears for yourself and others. The gift of bringing comfort to others in their grief. The gift on being nonjudgmental with others. The gift of allowing you to continue on with the most precious gift you have—your life.

Revere your memories
Bring into being new ones
Celebrate the life of your loved one
Celebrate your gift!

Resources

American Psychiatric Association. *Diagnostic and Statistical Manual of Mental Disorders*. Third Edition. Washington, D.C.: American Psychiatric Association Press, 1987. 113.

Atwater, P.M.H. *Beyond the Light*. New York, NY: Avon Books, 1994.

Bache, Christopher M. "A Perinatal Interpretation of Frightening Near-Death Experiences: A Dialogue with Kenneth Ring." *JNDS* 13 (1) (Fall 1994): 25-45.

Bailey, Lee W. and Jenny Yates. *The Near-Death Experience. A Reader*. New York [u.a.]: Routledge, 1996.

Barnett, Linda. "Hospice Nurses' Knowledge and Attitudes Toward the Near-Death Experience." *JNDS* 9 (4) (Summer 1991): 225-232.

Barrett, Sir William. *Death-Bed Visions*. London: Methuen, 1926.

Becker, Carl B. "A Philosopher's View of Near-Death Research." *JNDS* 14 (1) (Fall 1995): 17-27.

Bowlby, J. *Loss: Sadness and Depression*. New York, NY: Penquin, 1981.

Boykoff Schoenbeck, Susan, and Gerald D. Hocutt. "Near-Death Experiences in Patients Undergoing Cardiopulmonary Resuscitation." *JNDS* 9 (4) (Summer 1991): 211-218.

Clark, E. J. "Bereaved Persons Have Rights That Should Be Respected." *Principles of Thanatology*. Eds. A. Kutscher, A. Carr, & L. Kutscher. New York, NY: Columbia University Press, 1987.

Colgrove, M., H. Bloomfield, and P. McWilliams. *How to Survive the Loss of a Love*. Los Angeles, CA: Prelude Press, 1991.

Gerritsen, J.C., and P.C. Van der Ende. "The Development of a Care-Giving Burden Scale." *Age and Aging*. 23 (1994): 483-491.

Gibbs, John C. "Moody's Versus Siegel's Interpretation of the Near-Death Experience: An Evaluation Based on Recent Research." *Anabiosis-The Journal for Near- Death Studies* 5 (2) (1986): 67-82.

Gibson, Arvin S. *Echoes From Eternity*. Bountiful, UT: Horizon Publishers & Distributors, 1993.

Graves, S. *Expressions of Healing: Embracing the Process of Grief*. North Hollywood, CA: Newcastle, 1994.

Hinsie, L., and R. Campbell. *Psychiatric Dictionary*. Fourth Edition. New York, NY: Oxford University Press, 1970.

Kastenbaum, Robert and Beatrice. *Encyclopedia of Death*. Oryx Press, 1989.

Kubler-Ross, Elisabeth. *On Death and Dying*. New York, NY: Macmillian Publishing Co., 1969.

Lindemann, E. "Symptomatology and Management of Acute Grief." *American Journal of Psychiatry*. 101 (1944): 141-148.

Moody, Raymond A. *Life After Life: The Investigation of a Phenomenon—Survival of Bodily Death*. New York, NY: Bantam Books, 1977.

Nuland, Sherwin B. *How We Die*. New York, NY: Alfred A. Knopf, 1994.

Osis, Karlis and Erlendur Haraldsson. *At the Hour of Death*. Norwalk, Conn: Hastings House, 1997.

Parkes, Dr. Colin. *Bereavement in Adult Life*.

Rando, T.A. *Grieving.: How to Go On Living When Someone You Love Dies*. New York, NY: D.C. Heath and Company, 1988.

Ring, Kenneth. "The Impact of Near-Death Experiences on Persons Who Have Not Had Them: A Report of a Preliminary Study and Two Replications." *JNDS* 13 (4) (Summer 1995): 223-235.

Rosen, David H. *Transforming Depression*. New York, NY: G.P. Putnam & Sons, 1993.

Serdahely, William J. "Questions for the Dying Brain Hypothesis." *JNDS* 15 (1) (Fall 1996): 41-53.

Siegel, Ronald K. "The Psychology of Life After Death." *The Near-Death Experience: Problems, Prospects, Perspectives.*

Tillich, Paul. *The Dynamics of Faith*. New York, NY: Harper and Row, 1957.

Worden, J. W. *Grief Counseling and Grief Therapy*. New York, NY: Springer Publishing Co., 1991.

Zisook, S., R.A. Devaul, and M.A. Click, Jr. "Measuring Symptoms of Grief and Bereavement." *Am J Psychiatry*. 139 (1982): 1590-1593.

Printed in the United States
1259200001B/157-163